First Steps in English Linguistics
2nd Edition

影山太郎／ブレント・デ・シェン／日比谷潤子／ドナ・タツキ
Taro Kageyama / Brent de Chene / Junko Hibiya / Donna Tatsuki

英語
言語学の
第一歩

本書の本文および関連事項を録音した音声を、下記のウェブページからご利用いただけます。
- 第18刷以降、付属 CD に代えてウェブページでの音声提供となりました。
- 本書内で「CD」のアイコンがある箇所についても、CD ではなくウェブページからの音声利用となります。
- 音声は無断で複製・頒布したり、改変したりしないでください。

■音声掲載ページ

https://www.9640.jp/books_277/

※ URL はブラウザのアドレスバーに直接入力してください。

■パスワード

fseng77P

※半角英数字。大文字 / 小文字は正確に入力してください。

Preface

　国公私立をとわず，日本中の大学・短大で改革の嵐が吹き荒れ，伝統的な英文学科の多くが「コミュニケーション」「国際」「文化」「情報」などの言葉を含む名称に看板を掛け替えています。しかしながら，看板が新しくなったとしても，そこで研究・教育される学問の中身は一朝一夕に変わるものではありません。いやむしろ，学問が多様化し学際化すればするほど，拠り所となる確固たる礎が必要なはずです。また，現実問題として，英語教職の免許取得のためには英語学概論などの基礎的科目がひきつづき重要な意義を持っています。

　そのような社会状況の中で，本書は「英語言語学の第一歩」という表題にし，本文も英文で提示することにしました。「英語学」ではなく「英語言語学」としたのは，英語を中心的な対象としながらも，あくまで「一般言語学，理論言語学」という幅広い学問の一部であることを明確に表現したかったからです。さらに言えば，一般的な用語としても，「英語学」という呼称の代わりに「英語言語学」という名前が定着してほしいと希望しています。「言語学」という名前を表に出すことによって，英語学というものが単なる英語の勉強ではなく，人間というものの性質を総合的に捉えようとする＜認知科学＞の一部を構成するという意識をもたらしてくれると思います。また，本文を英文で執筆したのは，学生の英語力を向上させるだけでなく，国際化の中で，ひごろから英語で考え，英語で発表するための素地を作りたいと思ったからです。

　本書の特色は次のようにまとめられます。

- 英語学・言語学がまったく初めての一年生にも分かりやすく，英語言語学の全体像を紹介する。
- 統語論，意味論，形態論，音声学・音韻論，語用論のほか，英語史，社会言語学，心理言語学，応用言語学の全領域をカバーし，最初の章から最後の章までがスムーズな流れで読み通せるような構成を工夫した。
- 本文がやさしい英語で書かれていて，講義にも講読にも使える。
- 内容の理解を確認するための Comprehension Check と，本文の内容を深め発展させるための Exercises を付け，学生の主体的な学習を促す。
- 幾つかの Exercises では，インターネットのコーパスを使って用例集めの練習をする。
- 本文および関連事項を録音した音声を付け，耳からも理解を深める。

本書には，学生が読むべき参考書は載せていません。本書が終わった次の段階としては，西光義弘（編）『日英語対照による英語学概論』（くろしお出版）およびそこに引用されている参考書に進んでください。

　本書は4名の共著となっています。全体の構想を影山が作ったあと，次のようにチャプターを分担・執筆し，最後に，全体にわたって英語の文章を de Chene が整えました。

1　Why Study English Linguistics（影山）
2　How English Has Changed over the Centuries（de Chene；練習問題　影山）
3　How Words Are Made: Morphology（影山）
4　How Words Mean: Semantics I（影山）
5　How English Phrases Are Formed: Syntax I（de Chene；補足と練習　影山）
6　How English Sentences Are Formed: Syntax II（de Chene；補足　影山）
7　How Sentences Mean: Semantics II（影山）
8　How to Communicate with Other People: Pragmatics（影山）
9　The Sounds of English: Phonetics and Phonology（de Chene；練習問題　影山）
10　Regional Varieties of English: Sociolinguistics I（日比谷）
11　English in Society: Sociolinguistics II（日比谷）
12　How English Is Acquired: Psycholinguistics（日比谷・影山）
13　How English as a Second/Foreign Language Is Acquired: Applied Linguistics（Tatsuki）

　付属音声には，第1, 2章(p.19含む)，第3章の p.22-p.25，第8章の p.96-p.98，第9章，第11章が録音されています。
　吹き込みは，第1～3章は Ms. Maia Field，第9章は Dr. Brent de Chene，第11章の Cockney（コクニー）は Dr. John C. Maher，その他の章と p.19 は Dr. Judith May Newton にお願いしました。Cockney 以外はアメリカ英語です。

　最初にくろしお出版から本書の企画を依頼されてから4年以上も経ってしまいました。編集部の狩野晶子さんのご協力に感謝いたします。

2004年3月

Contents

Preface i

Chapter 1   Why Study English Linguistics 1
Knowledge of Language 1
What Is English Linguistics? 3
Components of Grammar 3
How English Has Been Studied 5
    Comprehension Check 6
    Exercises 6
    現代理論言語学の発展 8

Chapter 2   How English Has Changed over the Centuries 9
Three Stages in the History of English 9
Layers of Vocabulary 10
The Prehistory of English 10
The Old English Period 11
The Middle English Period 13
The Modern English Period 14
Sound Change 14
Morphological and Syntactic Change 15
    Comprehension Check 17
    Exercises 18
    これって，ほんとに英語なの？ 19

Chapter 3   How Words Are Made: Morphology 21
Dividing Words into Parts 21
Compounding 22
Derivation 25
Conversion 26
Inflection 27
Minor Word Formation Processes 28
    逆形成 29
    Comprehension Check 30
    Exercises 30

Chapter 4 How Words Mean: Semantics I 33
Kinds of Meaning.. 33
Meaning as a Set of Properties... 34
Categorization and Prototypes.. 35
Semantic Networks... 36
Synonyms and Antonyms 37
Polysemy 38
Metaphor and Metonymy 39
    Comprehension Check 41
    Exercises 41
    コトバの価値判断 43

Chapter 5 How English Phrases Are Formed: Syntax I 45
What Is Syntax?.. 45
Tests for Constituency.. 46
Complements and Adjuncts 48
Cross-categorial Parallelism... 49
Labeled Bracketings and Tree Diagrams 50
Retrospect and Prospect.. 51
    本文の理解を助けるために 53
    Comprehension Check 59
    Exercises 59

Chapter 6 How English Sentences Are Formed: Syntax II ... 63
Auxiliary Verbs, Tense, and the Tense Element t 63
Complex Sentences, the Element c, and Movement.............. 65
The Internal Structure of the Sequence of Sub-clausal Elements........... 67
Clause Structure and Historical Word-Order Change............. 69
    本文の理解を助けるために 71
    Comprehension Check 75
    Exercises 75

Chapter 7 How Sentences Mean: Semantics II 79
Semantic Roles and Argument Structure................................ 79
Selectional Restrictions 82
Constructional Meaning 82
Word Order and Information... 84
What Do Pronouns Refer to?.. 85

　　　　Comprehension Check 88
　　　　Exercises 88

Chapter 8　How to Communicate with Other People: Pragmatics ..93
　　What Is Pragmatics? 93
　　Formal vs. Informal Style 93
　　Politeness 94
　　Speech Acts 96
　　Conversational Implicature 97
　　The Co-operative Principle 98
　　　　Comprehension Check 100
　　　　Exercises 100
　　　　言葉にならない言葉 102

Chapter 9　The Sounds of English: Phonetics and Phonology 103
　　Sound and Meaning 103
　　Intonation 103
　　Word Accent and Syllable Structure 104
　　Vowels and Consonants 107
　　　　Comprehension Check 110
　　　　Exercises 111
　　　　長い母音の発音 113

Chapter 10　Regional Varieties of English: Sociolinguistics I 115
　　Englishes in the World 115
　　Regional Dialects 116
　　Intranational Variation 117
　　International Variation 119
　　　　Comprehension Check 123
　　　　Exercises 123
　　　　ニューヨークかヌーヨークか？ 125

Chapter 11　English in Society: Sociolinguistics II 127
　　Social Variation 127
　　Standard vs. Nonstandard English 127
　　Grammatical Variation 128
　　Phonological Variation 132
　　Lexical Variation 134

Language and Gender 134
    Comprehension Check 137
    Exercises 137
    いわゆる「黒人英語」という呼び名について 139

Chapter 12　How English Is Acquired: Psycholinguistics ... 141

First Language Acquisition 141
Phonological Development 141
Morphological Development 143
Syntactic Development 144
Semantic and Lexical Development 146
Theories of Language Acquisition 147
    Comprehension Check 150
    Exercises 150
    英語の分かるサル ── カンジ 152

Chapter 13　How English as a Second/Foreign Language Is Acquired: Applied Linguistics 153

Second Language Acquisition 153
Characteristics of Learner Language 153
Learner Progress 154
Influences Outside the Learner 155
Individual Differences among Learners 156
    Comprehension Check 159
    Exercise 159

Chapter 1 Why Study English Linguistics

> **BASIC QUESTIONS**
> English linguistics(英語言語学，つまり英語学)というのは，どういう学問なのだろうか。高校までの英語の勉強と，どう違うのだろう。それを勉強すると，どのような発見があるのだろうか。

KNOWLEDGE OF LANGUAGE CD Track 2

You may wonder why a 5-year-old American child can speak English far better than a Japanese university student who has studied the language for more than 6 years. Although we take it for granted, it's actually quite amazing that children can master a language at a very early age without being trained at school. This is not a matter of country, race, or intelligence. Any human being can acquire natural English if brought up in an environment where it is spoken, and this is true not only of English but of all human languages. Animals, however, are unable to achieve the miracle of **language acquisition**.

language acquisition = 言語の獲得，言語習得

Of course, this doesn't mean that children born into an English-speaking environment start to speak perfect English as soon as they are born. Children start out by "babbling" and at a later stage make "mistakes" like *goed* for *went* and *foots* for *feet*—a phenomenon called **overgeneralization** (Chapter 12). Interestingly, almost all English-speaking children make this kind of mistake at about the same age (3 or 4 years old) no matter where they are raised. This is parallel to the fact that almost all Japanese children, at about the same age, overgeneralize the use of の and say things like 赤い<u>の</u>服 instead of 赤い服 or パパが買った<u>の</u>ネクタイ instead of パパが買ったネクタイ. It is fascinating that such overgeneralizations are observed quite consistently among children who are in the process of acquiring their first language.

babble = 喃語(意味のない音声)を発する

overgeneralization = 過剰一般化

As the result of acquiring a language in childhood, speakers come to have a complex system of knowledge about that language. As an example of this knowledge, consider the meaning

phrase＝句	
interpretation＝解釈	

of the English phrase *old men and women*. This phrase can be understood in two ways, depending on what group of people *old* is taken to apply to. In one interpretation, *old* applies to both *men* and *women*, as indicated by the grouping [old [men and women]]. In the other, *old* applies only to *men*, as indicated by the grouping [[old men] and women]. **Native speakers** of English, even children, can detect the **ambiguity** of such a phrase—that is, the fact that it has two meanings that result from different groupings of words or "syntactic structures" (Chapter 5). However, there is no evidence that chimpanzees or other animals have the ability to understand such multiple meanings.

native speaker＝母語話者(幼児のときからその言語を自然に身につけた人)
ambiguity＝曖昧性
syntactic structure＝統語構造

The linguist Noam Chomsky regards facts like these as evidence that human beings are born with a special capacity for acquiring language (**Universal Grammar** or the **language faculty**). One more piece of evidence supporting the idea that the human language faculty is **innate** is the fact that the grammatical system of a language is amazingly uniform across native speakers, in spite of the fact that the input to language acquisition presumably varies a good deal from individual to individual.

Noam Chomsky＝ノウム・チョムスキー

Universal Grammar (UG)＝普遍文法(人間が生まれながらにして持っている言語能力)
language faculty＝言語能力
innate＝生得的な

It is true that there are many differences among the geographical and social dialects of a language like English (see Chapters 10 and 11), but these are not so great as to compromise the essential unity of the language. All speakers of English say *two big apples* rather than *big two apples, regardless of their age, birthplace, or social status, where an **asterisk** (*) in front of an example shows that it is not acceptable English. (This particular restriction on word order is in fact rather surprising, because a speaker of Japanese does not care about whether "two" or "big" comes first in the equivalent phrase: 2つの大きいリンゴ and 大きい2つのリンゴ are both possible.) This English word order restriction, of course, is not limited to *two* and *big*. Native speakers know the "general rule" that **numbers** always come before **adjectives**, and this is just one example of their **internalized** linguistic knowledge. The puzzle is how children acquire such an enormous and complex

asterisk＝アスタリスク，星印(その表現が非文法的であることを示す記号(言語学の慣習))

number＝数詞
adjective＝形容詞
internalize＝習得して自分のものにする

body of knowledge concerning their language. There must be
abstract principles that make this feat possible.

abstract principle=
抽象的な原理

WHAT IS ENGLISH LINGUISTICS?  Track 3

Linguistics is the scientific study of human language and aims to
discover the following:

linguistics＝言語学

(a) the nature of native speaker knowledge of language
(b) how this knowledge is acquired by children
　　(language acquisition)
(c) how this knowledge is used in actual contexts
　　(language use)

As a branch of linguistics, **English linguistics** tries to solve these
problems by focusing on English. Although the term *English
linguistics* is commonly translated into Japanese as 英語学, this
word should be taken to mean 英語言語学, and not a kind of 語学
(training of practical skills in English).

English linguistics＝英語
言語学，英語学

　Because language is very complex, linguistics has many subfields. The basic elements of language are **words**. You know
how to pronounce the three words *like*, *milk*, and *cats*, and what
each of them means. But that is not enough knowledge to predict
the form of a **sentence** involving these three words. If you were
asked to make such a sentence, you would say *Cats like milk*, and
not *Milk like cats or *Cats milk like. There is a rule for putting
the words in the right order. Words, sounds, meanings, and sentence composition are the essential components of the native
speakers' linguistic knowledge, called **grammar**.

subfield＝下位分野
word＝語，単語

sentence＝文

sound＝音声
meaning＝意味

grammar＝文法

COMPONENTS OF GRAMMAR  Track 4

● **morphology**: how words are made (→Chapter 3)
● **semantics**: how words and sentences are understood
　(→Chapters 4 and 7)
● **syntax**: how words are combined into phrases and sentences
　(→Chapters 5 and 6)
● **phonetics** and **phonology**: how words and sentences are
　pronounced (→Chapter 9)

morphology＝形態論
semantics＝意味論

syntax＝統語論

phonetics＝音声学
phonology＝音韻論

school grammar=
学校文法

The "grammar" referred to here is different from the "grammar" you studied in high school. **School grammar** is written in reference books and must be memorized, while the grammar you are going to study in this book is in the mind of native speakers and the researcher must discover what it is.

The four components of grammar listed above can also be considered subfields of linguistics. Further subfields are concerned with the relation of linguistic research to other areas of inquiry, as shown in Figure 1. Of these, **pragmatics**, **sociolinguistics**, **psycholinguistics**, **applied linguistics**, and **historical linguistics** are explained in the chapters indicated.

pragmatics = 語用論

sociolinguistics = 社会言語学

psycholinguistics = 心理言語学

historical linguistics = 歴史言語学

applied linguistics = 応用言語学

contrastive linguistics = 対照言語学

computational linguistics = 計算言語学

neurolinguistics = 神経言語学

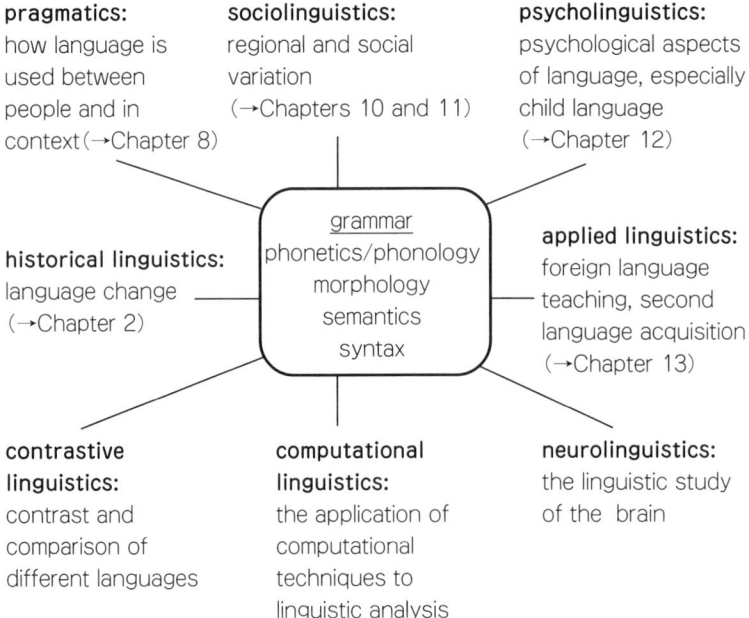

pragmatics: how language is used between people and in context (→Chapter 8)

sociolinguistics: regional and social variation (→Chapters 10 and 11)

psycholinguistics: psychological aspects of language, especially child language (→Chapter 12)

historical linguistics: language change (→Chapter 2)

grammar
phonetics/phonology
morphology
semantics
syntax

applied linguistics: foreign language teaching, second language acquisition (→Chapter 13)

contrastive linguistics: contrast and comparison of different languages

computational linguistics: the application of computational techniques to linguistic analysis

neurolinguistics: the linguistic study of the brain

Figure 1 Subfields of linguistics

A look at Figure 1 will convince you that linguistics is a broad and important area of study whose aim is to contribute to the understanding of human nature through the investigation of language. Linguistics thus has the potential to contribute not only to the understanding of language itself but also to various practical tasks involving language, such as foreign language teaching (**applied linguistics**), cross-linguistic and cross-cultural understanding (**contrastive linguistics**), the development of machine translation systems (**computational linguistics**), the treatment of language disorders (**neurolinguistics**), and so on.

HOW ENGLISH HAS BEEN STUDIED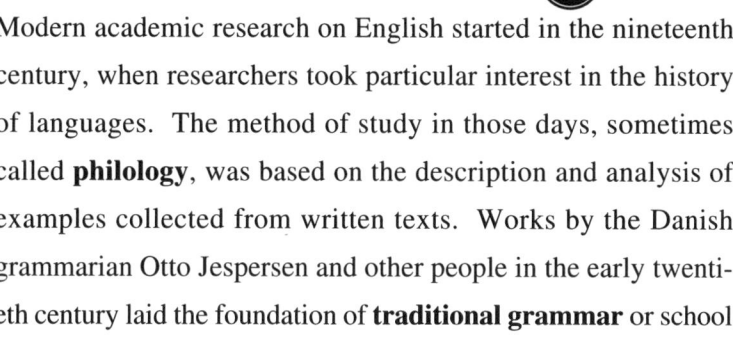

Modern academic research on English started in the nineteenth century, when researchers took particular interest in the history of languages. The method of study in those days, sometimes called **philology**, was based on the description and analysis of examples collected from written texts. Works by the Danish grammarian Otto Jespersen and other people in the early twentieth century laid the foundation of **traditional grammar** or school grammar.

philology = 文献学

Otto Jespersen = オットー・イェスペルセン
traditional grammar = 伝統文法

Meanwhile, scholars began to shift their attention from language history to the state of individual languages at a given point in time. In the first half of the twentieth century, **structural linguistics** grew out of work by Ferdinand de Saussure in Europe and by Edward Sapir and Leonard Bloomfield in the U.S.A.

structural linguistics = 構造言語学
Ferdinand de Saussure = フェルディナン・ド・ソシュール
Edward Sapir = エドワード・サピア
Leonard Bloomfield = レナード・ブルームフィールド
generative grammar = 生成文法

When structural linguistics reached an impasse, a revolutionary breakthrough was achieved by the American linguist Noam Chomsky in his book *Syntactic Structures* (1957). Chomsky's theory, called **generative grammar**, has become very influential, and he and his co-workers have made numerous discoveries about the universal principles of language as well as about the details of English and other languages. Chomsky's ideas have not been accepted in full by all language researchers, and people who have found unproductive his idea of isolating the study of grammar from the study of language use have developed approaches to language that emphasize the relation between language and the psychological and perceptual abilities of human beings (**cognitive linguistics**) or the actual use of language (pragmatics, sociolinguistics, **corpus linguistics**). But it is most reasonable to regard these different approaches as complementary to each other rather than mutually exclusive.

cognitive linguistics = 認知言語学
corpus linguistics = コーパス言語学

Comprehension Check

✎ (　　　) には日本語を，＿＿＿＿＿＿ には英語を補いなさい。

「英語学」というのを英語で言うと＿＿＿＿＿＿であり，これは「英語の(　　　)」という意味である。英語学の最終目標は，英語という言語の研究を通して，(a)人間の(　　　)がどのようなものであるのかを解明し，さらに，(b)幼児の言語(　　　)の過程と，(c)さまざまな状況における言語の実際の(　　　)を明らかにすることである。Chomsky によれば，人間は，(　　　)文法と呼ばれる，他の動物には見られない言語習得能力を(　　　)的に持っている。Chomsky の(　　　)文法理論では，言語能力はそれだけで自律的に存在すると見なされるが，他方，(　　　)言語学では，言語能力はそれだけで独立に成り立つのではなく，人間の心理的，知覚的機構と直結していると考えられている。いずれにしても，現在の英語学は，実用的な英語の訓練でないことは言うまでもないが，昔の英語の歴史的な資料を研究した(　　　)とも，考え方が根本的に異なるのである。

Exercises

(1) 1〜10 に示す事柄は，英語言語学の中のどの専門領域に属する問題と考えられますか。枠内に示した分野名から，それぞれ 1 つ選びなさい。

> ● 音声学(phonetics)　● 形態論(morphology)　● 統語論(syntax)
> ● 意味論(semantics)　● 語用論(pragmatics)
> ● 応用言語学(applied linguistics)　● 心理言語学(psycholinguistics)
> ● 社会言語学(sociolinguistics)　● 歴史言語学(historical linguistics)

1. 英語の文法では，疑問文を作るときに，What did John buy at the store ? や Where did John buy it? のように，what や where という疑問詞を文の先頭に置き，その後に do/did を付ける。(　　　　　)

2. 男性のことばと女性のことばを比べると，I like it so much. や He was so sweet. のように，so で強調するのは男性より女性のほうが多い。(　　　　　)

3. "of" という前置詞の "f" は普通なら [v] と発音するが，of course というときには，[f] という音になることが多い。同様に，"news" の最後の "s" は普通なら [z] と発音するが，newspaper という言葉では [s] になることが多い。
(　　　　　)

4. large と big は同じような意味を表すことばで類義語と呼ばれるが，large と small は反対の意味を表す反義語である。（　　　　　）

5. ネイティヴスピーカの幼児が英語を身につける過程を観察すると，run の過去形を runned と言ったり，Daddy came. を Came daddy. と言ったりすることがある。（　　　　　）

6. ことばの使い方は話し相手によって変わる。初対面のあいさつで，目上の人には How do you do, Mr. Smith? のように言うのが礼儀正しいが，学生同志が紹介されたような場合には，Hi, Tom! で充分である。（　　　　　）

7. 私は将来，英語教師を志望していて，言語学の理論を中学・高校の英語教育の現場で実際に応用することに興味がある。（　　　　　）

8. 世界中の英語は決して画一的ではない。ネイティヴスピーカでも，地域や階層によっては，三人称単数現在形の-sを使わないで，He go there. のように言うことがある。（　　　　　）

9. １つの単語から別の単語を作るとき，happy（幸せな）の名詞形は -ness を付けて happiness とするが，long（長い）の名詞形は longness ではなく，length とする。（　　　　　）

10. 関係代名詞の歴史的発達を調べると，英語の一番古い時代には，that に当たるものしかなかったが，中世になると who や which も使われるように変化してきたことが分かる。（　　　　　）

(2) 動物の鳴き声や蜜蜂のダンスは，仲間に何らかの信号を送る働きをすると言われているが，その信号は基本的に幾つかのパターンに限られる。これに対して，人間の言語の語彙数は膨大であり，英語だけでも十数万の単語があると言われる。人間と動物で語彙の数が違うのは，脳の物理的な容量が違うためであると考えられるかも知れない。しかし Chomsky は，人間の言語と動物の信号は，量だけでなく根本的な質が違うと考え，このことを示すために，次のようなことを指摘した。この例から，人間の言語はどのような点で特別だと言えるだろうか。

  a. John loves Mary.
  b. Bill thinks John loves Mary.
  c. Sue believes Bill thinks John loves Mary.
  d. I suspect Sue believes Bill thinks John loves Mary.　等々

現代理論言語学の発展

現代の理論言語学の中でも中心となる統語論・意味論の領域で，代表的な理論がどのように発達し，どのように互いに関係しているかを図解しておく（太字は理論の固有名。文献はすべてチョムスキーによる）。

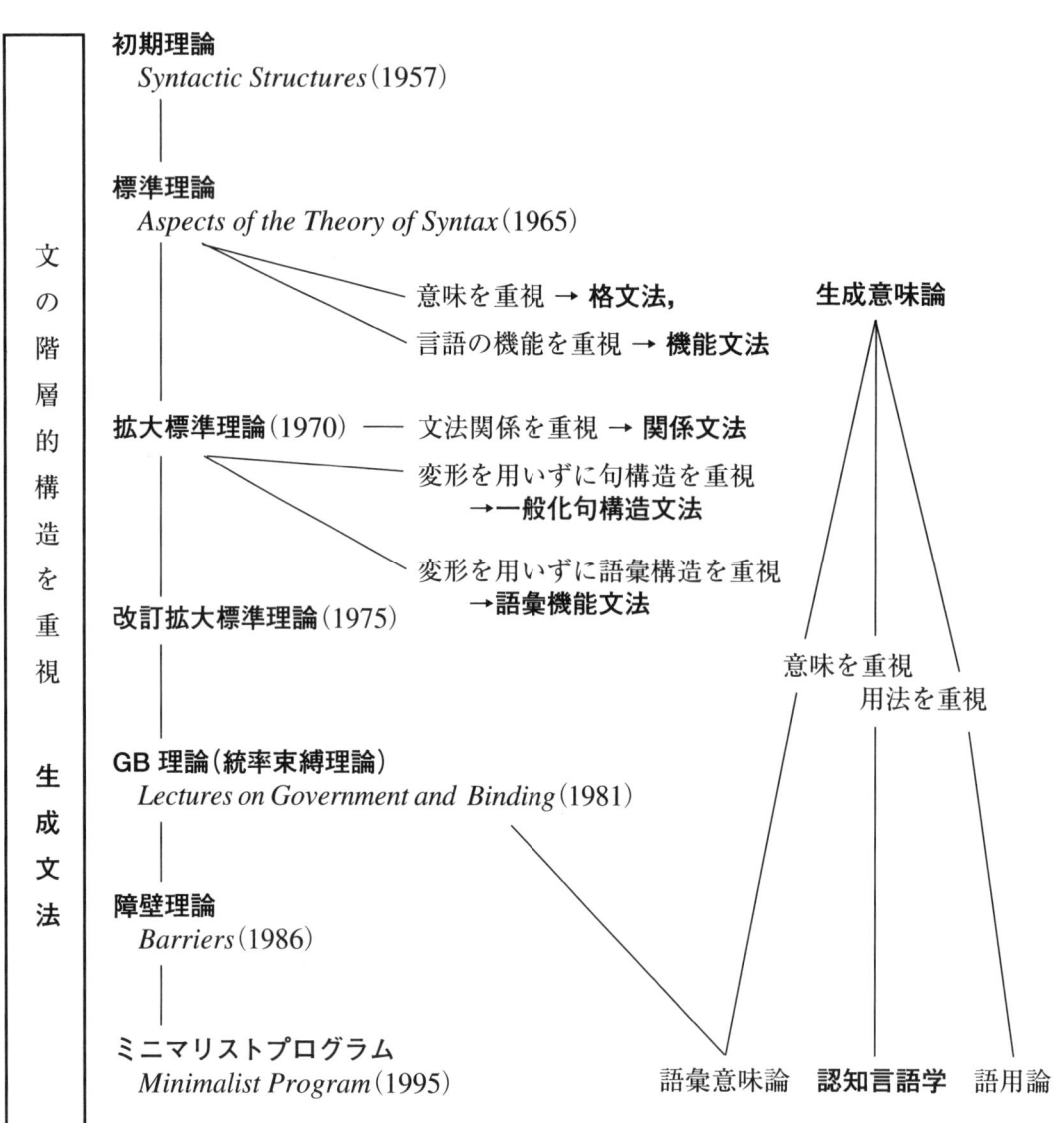

Chapter 2 How English Has Changed over the Centuries

> **BASIC QUESTIONS**
> いまや英語は世界各地で話されているが，そのルーツはどこから来ているのだろうか。英語はいつ頃から始まり，どのように変化してきたのだろうか。昔の英語は，今の私たちでも理解できるのだろうか。日本語には「和語」，「漢語」，「外来語」の違いがあるが，英語にもそのような違いがあるのだろうか。

THREE STAGES IN THE HISTORY OF ENGLISH CD Track 6

The English language has a written history of thirteen or fourteen centuries. During that period, it has undergone many changes that have drastically affected its phonology (sound structure), morphology (word structure), and syntax (sentence structure). The gap between the English of the oldest documents, which date from the late 7th century, and the contemporary language is so great that modern speakers must study the earliest English essentially as a foreign language.

The history of English is typically divided into three major periods.

Old English (OE): 650 — 1100
Middle English (ME): 1100 — 1500
Modern English (ModE): 1500 —

Old English＝古英語
Middle English＝中英語
Modern English＝近代英語

This classification is based on features such as **pronunciation**, **inflectional endings**, and **word order**. Old English is characterized by a complex system of endings on **nouns** and **verbs** and considerable freedom in the order of words. In Middle English, many of the endings which showed **grammatical relations** such as **subject** and **object** were lost and, to compensate for the loss, the word order of subject, object, and verb became fixed. The transition to Modern English is marked by a large-scale sound change called the **Great Vowel Shift**, which occurred for the most part during the 1400s. According to the above classification, contemporary English represents one stage of Modern English, but English since 1900 is sometimes called **Present-day English**.

pronunciation＝発音
inflectional endings＝屈折語尾
word order＝語順
noun＝名詞
verb＝動詞
grammatical relation＝文法関係(主語，目的語など)
subject＝主語
object＝目的語

Great Vowel Shift＝大母音推移

Present-day English＝現代英語

LAYERS OF VOCABULARY 🆑 Track 7

Although English and Japanese are completely unrelated in origin, they are similar in the way they have enriched their stock of words, or **lexicon**. The lexicon of English, much like that of Japanese, consists of a core of common words that date from prehistoric times, supplemented by several **strata** or **layers** of **borrowings** from other languages. In particular, the role of the **Greek** and (especially) **Latin** element in the English lexicon is very much parallel to the role of the Chinese element in the Japanese lexicon. As one illustration, consider the following example:

	native words		borrowed words
Japanese	なかば	しま	はん-とう
English	half	island	pen-insula
meaning	半	島	半島

Table 1 Similarity of English and Japanese Lexical Strata

In both English and Japanese, the meanings 「半」 and 「島」 are expressed with native words—words that, as far as we know, have always been part of their respective languages. These are **Germanic** or **Anglo-Saxon** words in the case of English and 大和ことば in the case of Japanese. The meaning 「半島」, on the other hand, is expressed by a word composed of borrowed elements, Chinese elements (漢語) in the case of Japanese and Latin elements in the case of English (the only inexact point of the comparison here is that the first element *pen-* < *paene* of *peninsula* means 'almost' rather than 'half' in Latin).

THE PREHISTORY OF ENGLISH 🆑 Track 8

English is a member of the **Germanic** group of languages, whose other major members are Dutch, German, Icelandic, Danish, Norwegian, and Swedish. Germanic itself is one branch of the **Indo-European language family**, which includes not only most languages of Europe (e.g. Irish, French, Spanish, Italian, Greek, Russian, Polish, and Serbian/Croatian/Bosnian) but also languages of India (Hindi, Bengali, and many others), Iran, Albania, and Armenia. Because the prehistory of the Indo-European language family can be reconstructed by comparing the oldest existing members of the family, many aspects of the prehistory of English are relatively well understood.

 A significant part of the English lexicon, including many words for concepts such as body parts (e.g. *tooth* and *heart*), kinship relations (e.g. *mother* and *brother*), and the numbers from one to ten, can be traced back to **Proto-Indo-European**, the unwritten ancestor of all Indo-European languages. Proto-Indo-European was spoken roughly five thousand years ago, perhaps in what is now southern Russia. A second core layer in the English lexicon is composed of words like *blood*, *bone*, and *sea*. These occur throughout the Germanic languages and must be attributed to **Proto-Germanic**, spoken about 750 B.C. in southern Scandinavia. They are unknown outside Germanic, however, and thus may represent at least in part loanwords from non-Indo-European sources.

reconstruct＝再建する

Proto-Indo-European＝
インド・ヨーロッパ祖語

Proto-Germanic＝
ゲルマン祖語

THE OLD ENGLISH PERIOD  Track 9

Around the year 400 A.D., speakers of three closely related Germanic dialects spoken in what is now southern Denmark and the northernmost part of Germany began a series of attacks on the island we know as Great Britain that, by roughly one hundred years later, put them in control of most of present-day England. These were the **Angles**, the **Saxons**, and the **Jutes**, and their language, with its various dialects, is the ancestor of modern English. (The name *England* comes from Old English *Engla-land* 'land of the Angles'.) These Germanic tribes, of course, did not find Great Britain unpopulated. The pre-Germanic inhabitants were for the most part speakers of **Celtic** languages —specifically, languages of the **Brythonic** or British branch of Celtic, of which modern **Welsh** is a representative. The language of the Germanic invaders, however, was so dominant in the territory

dialect＝方言

Angles＝アングル人
Saxons＝サクソン人
Jutes＝ジュート人

Celtic＝ケルト語派
Brythonic＝ブリトン語派
Welsh＝ウェールズ語

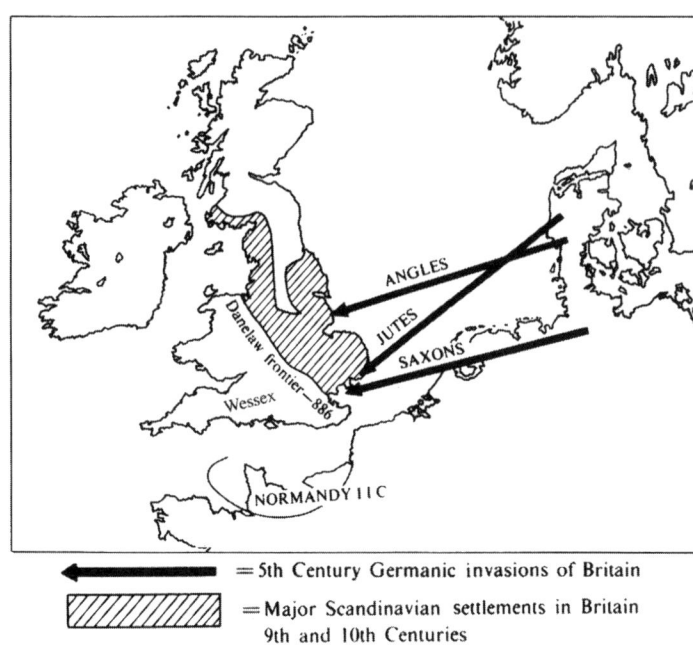

= 5th Century Germanic invasions of Britain

= Major Scandinavian settlements in Britain 9th and 10th Centuries

they controlled that the lexicon of English shows virtually no influence from Celtic languages.

The linguistic state of England had been essentially stable for about three centuries when, shortly before the year 800, "Vikings" or Danish forces began a series of attacks whose goal gradually expanded from plunder to the establishment of permanent settlements. Eventually, the **Danes** aimed at the conquest of all England. At one point in the late 800s they came close to achieving this goal, but their expansion was stopped by the forces of **Alfred the Great**, originally the king of **Wessex**. The language of the Danes, known as **Old Norse**, exerted a significant influence on the English lexicon. For example, the Old Norse form *egg* competed with and gradually replaced the **cognate** native form *ei* (compare modern German *Ei*), where cognates are forms that come originally from the same word or root. In a similar development, English borrowed the Old Norse form *skirt*, cognate with the native form *shirt*. In this latter case, however, both forms have survived to the present day, and thus constitute **doublets** of each other—that is, words derived from the same source through

Danish = (下記 "Dane" の形容詞形)

Danes = デーン人 (北欧人)

Alfred the Great = アルフレッド大王
Wessex = ウェセックス王国
Old Norse = 古ノルド語 (古北欧語)
cognate = 同系語, 同族語

root = 語根

doublet = 姉妹語 (同じ語源から派生した異なる単語)

different routes of transmission. You may be surprised to learn that even words as basic as the forms of the **third person plural pronoun**, *they, their,* and *them,* which seem completely typical of English, originally come from Old Norse.

THE MIDDLE ENGLISH PERIOD

The influence of Old Norse on English, however, pales beside that of **Norman French**, which became the language of the upper classes and of law, administration, and the church after the **Norman Conquest** of 1066. The Normans were originally, like the Danes, Scandinavian pirates. They settled in northwestern France by about the year 900 and eventually adopted Christianity and the French language. Thus, when they invaded Great Britain under **William of Normandy**, the language they brought with them was French.

Words of French origin are pervasive in contemporary English, and it is hardly possible to write a sentence without using one or more of them. In the last paragraph, for example, the words *influence, pale, language, administer* (*administration*), *invasion,* and *original* (*originally*) are all borrowings into Middle English from **Old French**. The cultural difference between speakers of Old English and speakers of Norman French is suggested by the fact that words relating to government, justice, and religion are typically French, as are all three of these words themselves; the same is true for words relating to art, fashion, and cuisine (and, again, those three words). With respect to cuisine, it is a common observation that while farm animals retain their Old English names (*cow/ox, pig/swine, sheep*), the meat derived from them is typically indicated by a French word (*beef, pork, mutton*; note the Japanese parallel in 牛 versus 牛肉).

The greatest writer of the Middle English period was **Geoffrey Chaucer** (1343(?)—1400). By writing his *Canterbury Tales* and other works in colloquial English rather than in French, he contributed to establishing the English spoken in London as the standard language.

THE MODERN ENGLISH PERIOD CD Track 11

The flow of French loanwords into Middle English was greatest during the period from 1250 to about 1400. Toward the end of this period, the rediscovery of classical learning known as the **Renaissance** was gathering momentum, and the associated influx of Latin words proved the last great influence that has shaped the modern English lexicon. During the Renaissance, many words were borrowed directly from Latin even though French versions of them already existed; this gave rise to doublets such as *frail* and *fragile*, *strait* and *strict*, *sure* and *secure*, where in each case the first version is French while the second is closer to the original Latin. Similarly, many Greek words were borrowed, either directly or through Latin. The effect of massive borrowing from the classical languages was such that up to the present day, essentially the entire lexicon of Latin and Greek has remained accessible for the coining of new words, typically words relating to scientific or technological advances. Thus, words like *gene* (Gk. *gen-* 'birth, origin'), *clone* (Gk. *klōn* 'sprout, twig'), and **compounds** in *cyber-* (Gk. *kubern-* 'to steer, guide') are all formations of the twentieth century, and there is no question that the future will see more such **coinages**.

Over the last several centuries, English has borrowed words from many other languages as well, just as Japanese has incorporated a huge number of 外来語 since the 1500s. Examples of such **loanwords** in English are *karate* and *karaoke* (from Japanese), *mosquito* and *siesta* (from Spanish), *bamboo* and (rice) *paddy* (from Malay), *coffee* (from Arabic through Turkish and Italian), and *tea* (from Chinese, perhaps through Malay and Dutch).

SOUND CHANGE CD Track 12

While both the **vowels** and the **consonants** of English have undergone essentially continuous change since the earliest times,

Renaissance＝ルネサンス

compound＝複合語

coinage＝新造語

loanword＝借用語

vowel＝母音
consonant＝子音

the most significant sound change in the history of the language is probably the Great Vowel Shift, which had already begun in Chaucer's day and was essentially complete by the time of William Shakespeare (1564—1616).

William Shakespeare＝ウィリアム・シェイクスピア

In Old and Middle English, the vowel letters *a*, *e*, *i*, *o*, and *u* were pronounced [a:], [e:], [i:], [o:], and [u:], much as in modern German or Italian. As a result of the Great Vowel Shift, however, the **long vowels** of Middle English all changed. First, [i:] and [u:] (as in *life* [li:f] and *house* [hu:s]) became the **diphthongs** [aj] and [aw], respectively, that they are to this day. Similarly, [e:] and [o:] (as in *deed* [de:d] and *moon* [mo:n]), rose (i.e. came to be pronounced with a higher **tongue position**) and **diphthongized** to become [ij] and [uw]. The vowels [a:] and [ɔ:] (as in *name* [na:m] and *home* [hɔ:m]), finally, rose and diphthongized to become [ej] and [ow].

long vowel＝長母音

diphthong＝二重母音

tongue position＝舌の位置
diphthongize＝二重母音化する

MORPHOLOGICAL AND SYNTACTIC CHANGE ⓒⓓ Track 13

The grammar of Old English is characterized by inflectional endings on nouns, verbs, adjectives, and even **determiners**. For example, the noun *stone* had different endings depending on its **number** (**singular** or **plural**) and its **case** or grammatical relation (subject, **direct object**, **indirect object**, or **possessor**), as shown in Table 2 (the mark " ‾ " indicates a long sound):

determiner＝限定詞（冠詞，指示詞のこと）
number＝数
singular＝単数
plural＝複数
case＝格
direct object＝直接目的語
indirect object＝間接目的語
possessor＝所有者
nominative＝主格
accusative＝対格
dative＝与格
genitive＝属格

	singular	plural
nominative case (subject)	stān	stān-as
accusative case (direct object)	stān	stān-as
dative case (indirect object)	stān-e	stān-um
genitive case (possessor)	stān-es	stān-a

Table 2 An example of Old English noun inflection

Because of the information concerning grammatical relations provided by these endings, the order of words in an Old English sentence could be relatively free. With the disappearance of inflectional endings as the result of sound change, word order became more rigidly fixed.

As our final example of a grammatical change, let us look at some differences in word order between the English of Shakespeare's time and that of our own. First, note that in contemporary English a **main verb** (shown with a double underline in the examples below) must follow an **adverb** like *often*, the **negative** element *not*, or an **adverbial quantifier** like *all* (shown with a single underline); the opposite order is totally impossible in each case:

(1) a. Jim often drinks coffee. (*Jim drinks often coffee.)
    b. Sue does not drink coffee. (*Sue drinks not coffee.)
    c. The children all drink coffee. (≠The children drink all coffee.)

Up to the time of Shakespeare, however, precisely the opposite order was observed:

(2) a. And the erthe and the lond chaungeth often his colour.
       'And the earth and land often change their color.'
       (c.1400; Maundeville, *The buke of John Maundewille* ix.100 (*OED*))
    b. I think not of them. (1605; Shakespeare, *Macbeth* II,i,20)
    c. let them fly all: (1605; Shakespeare, *Macbeth* V,iii,1)

Similarly, while a main verb (double underline) appears to the right of the subject (single underline) in contemporary English **questions** (examples (3)), it typically appears to the left of the subject in questions for Shakespeare (examples (4)):

(3) a. Do you ride?
    b. What do I care?
(4) a. Ride you this afternoon? (1605; Shakespeare, *Macbeth* III,i,18)
    b. What care I, if .... (1605; Shakespeare, *Macbeth* III,iv,67)

In Chapter 6, we will see how all of these word-order differences between Shakespeare's English and our own have a simple and unified explanation.

---

main verb＝本動詞
adverb＝副詞
negative＝否定
adverbial quantifier＝副詞的数量詞

question＝疑問文

Comprehension Check

✏️ (　　)には日本語，＿＿＿＿には英語，[　]には発音記号を補いなさい。

　英語は，インド・ヨーロッパ語族の中の(　　　)語派に属し，もともとは，デンマークや北部ドイツに住んでいた民族の言葉である。すなわち，西暦450年頃に，(　　　)人，(　　　)人，(　　　)人というゲルマン民族がブリテン島に侵入し，先住民である(　　　)人を西のウェールズや北のスコットランドに追いやって，自分達の王国を築いた。Englandという名前は元来 Engla(Angla)-land つまり(　　　)という意味である。この最も古い時代の英語を＿＿＿＿と呼ぶ。その英語は，名詞・動詞・形容詞・冠詞などが複雑な(　　　)を持ち，むしろ現在のドイツ語と似ている。その代わり，(　　　)は比較的自由だった。8～9世紀には，ノルウェーやデンマークから(　　　)がイギリスを襲い，北部と東部を中心に国中を荒し回った。この民族から入ってきた単語には，shirtと姉妹語である＿＿＿＿や，egg, giveのような単語，そして＿＿＿＿, ＿＿＿＿, ＿＿＿＿という三人称複数代名詞などがある。この侵略者を食い止めて和睦にもちこんだのがWessex王国の(　　　)大王である。

　(　　　)年にはノルマンディー公(　　　)の率いる(　　　)人がイギリスの王位を主張して攻め入り，英国軍を破った。それ以後300年間は，王を始めとする宮廷の人々は(　　　)語を用い，政治，法律，服飾，芸術など様々な分野にわたって多数の(　　　)語が英語に入ってきた。しかし，英語は消滅したわけではなく，一般市民は英語を使っていたから，家畜とその食肉を表す単語(例えば＿＿＿＿と＿＿＿＿, ＿＿＿＿と＿＿＿＿)が各々，英語とフランス語に分かれるというおもしろい結果となった。この時代，つまり(　　　)年から(　　　)年までの英語を＿＿＿＿と言う。この時期の文法的な変化としては，以前は複雑だった名詞や動詞の(　　　)が簡略化され，それに伴って(　　　)が主語＋動詞＋目的語に固定されてきたことが挙げられる。この時代の最も有名な作家として，＿＿＿＿などを書いた＿＿＿＿がいる。彼は英語を文学に使える言語として高めただけでなく，それまで様々な方言に分かれていた英語の標準語の基礎を作った。

　15世紀ごろから(　　　)と呼ばれる大規模な発音の変化が起こった。これはアクセントのある(　　　)母音において舌の位置が次第に高くなっていったもので，例えば，nameの母音は[　]から最終的には[　]に，rideの母音は[　]から[　]に，houseの母音は[　]から[　]に，各々変化した。

　(　　　)年以降の英語は＿＿＿＿と呼ばれ，その初期には世界最大の劇作家である＿＿＿＿が活躍した。その当時の英語は，かなり現在の英語に近い姿になっていたが，それでもまだ，古い時代の名残りが見られ，"I don't drink."を＿＿＿＿

のように，"Do you ride this afternoon?" を＿＿＿＿のように表現していた。
「文芸復興」と呼ばれる＿＿＿＿の時代には（　　　）語と（　　　）語を基にして，多くの学術用語などが作られた。

Exercises

(1) 英語が所属する「インド・ヨーロッパ語族」の中の兄弟関係を図示すると，概略，次のようになる。空欄に該当する言語名を下の《　》から選んで入れなさい。

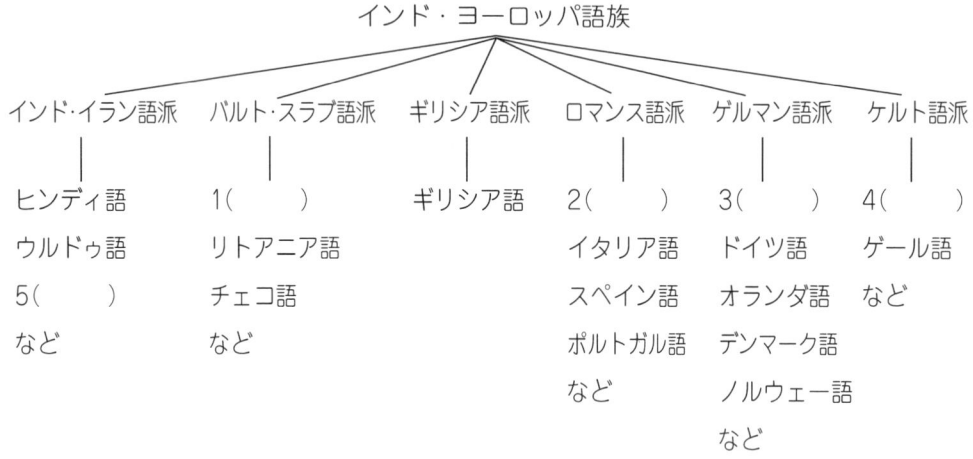

《英語，フランス語，ペルシア語，ウェールズ語，ロシア語》

(2) 次の単語がゲルマン系(本来の英語)か，ラテン系(フランス語からの借入)か判断しなさい。

【ヒント1】foot—feet，see—saw—seen のように母音を変えて不規則変化する名詞や動詞は，ゲルマン系に限られる。

【ヒント2】long—length のように，品詞が変わるときに母音が変わるのはゲルマン系である。

【ヒント3】動詞が名詞になるとき，いろいろな語尾が付くが，その中で-ment, -ance, -ion など語尾はラテン系である。

　　a. tooth　　　b. develop　　　c. strong　　　d. discuss
　　e. grow　　　f. attend

(3) 次の単語は元々どこの言語から来たものか，辞書で調べなさい。

　　a. robot　　　b. hospital　　　c. algebra　　　d. boomerang
　　e. igloo　　　f. piano　　　g. bungalow　　　h. cafeteria

(4) 辞書を参考にして，次の10個の単語を，2つずつの姉妹語のペアに分けなさい。

　　1. hostel　　　2. dish　　　3. secure　　　4. warranty

5. cattle　　　6. guarantee　　　7. capital　　　8. hotel
9. disc　　　10. sure

これって，ほんとに英語なの？  Track 14

昔の英語の一例として，新約聖書マタイ福音書の「主の祈りThe Lord's Prayer」の冒頭を見てみよう。

The Lord's Prayer（現代英語）

　　Our Father in heaven,　　　　　　　　天にいます私たちの父よ，
　　hallowed be your name,　　　　　　　御名があがめられますように。
　　your kingdom come,　　　　　　　　　御国が来ますように。
　　your will be done, on earth as in heaven.　みこころが天で行われるように地でも行われますように。
　　Give us today our daily bread.　　　　私たちの日ごとの糧をきょうもお与えください。

次の初期近代英語（1600年ごろ）では，art（be動詞の二人称単数現在形），thy（汝の）といった古い単語が出てくるし，vがuと綴られている。さらにもっと古い時代の英語は読むことも難しくなってくる。付属のCDの朗読で，数百年前の英語のおもむきを味わってみよう。

Early Modern English（初期近代英語）

　　Our father, which art in heauen,
　　hallowed be thy name.
　　Thy kingdome come,
　　Thy will be done, on earth as it is in heauen.
　　Giue us this day our daily bread.

Middle English（中英語）

　　Oure fadir
　　that art in heuenes,
　　halewid be thi name;
　　thi kyngdoom come to;
　　be thi wille don in erthe as in heuene;
　　ȝyue to vs this dai oure breed.

Old English（古英語）

　　Fæder ūre
　　þū þe eart on heofonum,
　　Si þin nama gehālgod.
　　Tōbecume þin rice.
　　Gewurþe ðin willa on eorðan swā swā on heofonum.
　　Urne gedæghwāmlican hlāf syle ūs tō dæg.

Chapter 3 How Words Are Made: Morphology

> **BASIC QUESTIONS**
> 高校生のときには英単語を丸暗記したが，単語の中身はどうなっているのだろうか。
> 単語は，どのような仕組みで作られるのだろうか。

DIVIDING WORDS INTO PARTS

Most **words** can be divided into smaller parts. Just as the Japanese 電話 is composed of 電 (electric) and 話 (talk), *telephone* is separated into two Greek elements, *tele-* ('far') and *-phone* ('sound, voice'). The smallest units of language that have a meaning are called **morphemes**. Words like *table* which cannot be divided any further consist of just one morpheme. If a morpheme can stand alone as a word, it is a **free** morpheme; otherwise, it is a **bound** morpheme. Morphology (also referred to as **word formation**) deals with how morphemes or words are joined to make up (larger) words.

word＝語（単語）

morpheme＝形態素

free morpheme＝
自由形態素
bound morpheme＝
拘束形態素
word formation＝語形成

Let us see how the following words are split into morphemes:

(1) book (2) bookstore (3) philosophy (4) apples (5) hopeless (6) unable
　　↓　　　　↓　　　　　　↓　　　　　　↓　　　　　↓　　　　　　↓
　 book　 book+store　 philo+sophy　 apple+s　 hope+less　 un+able

Book in (1) consists of one free morpheme. *Bookstore* in (2) is composed of two free morphemes, *book* and *store*. In (3), *philosophy* is divided into two bound morphemes, *philo-* (Greek for 'loving') and *-sophy* (Greek for 'wisdom'). The term *morphology* itself is made up of Greek elements (*morpho-* 'form' and *-logy* 'study, science'), as are many other academic terms.

In (4), *apple* is followed by the ending *-s*, which represents "plural." The *-s* is pronounced [z] in *apples*, but it has different pronunciations in *desks* and *benches*. Different forms (pronunciations) of the same morpheme are called **allomorphs** of that morpheme. "Allomorphic variation" is also found in the third person singular **present tense** verbal ending (*loves, kicks,*

allomorph＝異形態

present tense＝現在時制

catches) and the **past tense** ending (*smil<u>ed</u>, laugh<u>ed</u>, shout<u>ed</u>*). These endings, called **inflections**, change neither the basic lexical meaning of a word nor its **lexical category** (its **part of speech**). In contrast, *-less* in *hopeless* (5) affects both meaning and category. *Hope* is a noun with a positive meaning, while *hopeless* is an adjective with a negative meaning. In (6), there is no change of category, but the meaning has changed: *able* is positive but *unable* is negative. Morphemes like *-less* and *un-* serve to make new words by **derivation** (see below).

COMPOUNDING  Track 15

Compounding is the process of combining two words into a larger word, as *teaspoon* is made from *tea* and *spoon* and *homesick* from *home* and *sick*. (We are not concerned here with how compounds are spelled, whether with a space between the elements (*high school* (noun)), with a hyphen (*high-school* (adjective)), or without a space or hyphen (*highway*).) Compounding is such a simple process that children master it very early—earlier, in any case, than they learn to use **derivational** morphemes. Children up to three years old tend to say *cut-thing* or *build-man* instead of *cutter* or *builder*. Words like *philosophy* and *telephone* that consist of two bound morphemes of Greek or Latin origin are sometimes called **neo-classical compounds** to distinguish them from compounds of other types.

Compounds in English are typically pronounced with an accent or **stress** on the first member, as in *TEAspoon* instead of *teaSPOON* and *HOMEsick* instead of *homeSICK* (capital letters indicate primary stress). This rule, called the **Compound Stress Rule**, is often contrasted with the **Phrasal Stress Rule**, which puts a stress on the element at the end of a phrase, as in *pretty GIRLS* and (*Time*) *passed BY*. Table 1 illustrates the differences in meaning and stress pattern between compound words and **phrases**.

Compound words	Phrases
LOUDspeaker (スピーカー)	loud SPEAKER
BLUEbird (ツグミの一種)	blue BIRD
GREENhouse (温室)	green HOUSE
PUSHup (腕立て伏せ)	to push something UP

Table 1 Stress in compounds and phrases

However, the Compound Stress Rule has exceptions, particularly among compound adjectives involving a verbal suffix like *-en, -ed,* or *-ing*. Thus, *well-known, hard-working, open-minded,* and *soft-spoken* all have primary stress on the second member.

Compounds are formed on a principled basis. If the two nouns *kite* and *box* are put together in that order, you get a compound *KITE box*, interpreted as a box for storing kites. If the two words are combined in the reverse order, the result is the completely different compound *BOX kite*, which means a kind of kite that is shaped like a box. In both cases, the **head**, or the element that determines the basic properties of the whole compound, is the second or right-hand word. This is referred to as the **Right-hand Head Rule**.

Compounds that have a head are called **endocentric**, and the vast majority of them obey the Right-hand Head Rule. *Flower shop, coffee shop, gift shop,* and *beauty shop*, which share *shop* as the head, are all compound nouns referring to a kind of shop, and *homesick, seasick, airsick,* and *lovesick* are all compound adjectives meaning a kind of sickness. Some compounds, however, do not have a head, and are called **exocentric**. Consider for example the adjective-noun compounds *blackboard*(黒板) and *blackhead*(上部が黒いニキビ). A *blackboard* is a kind of board, and so *board* is clearly the head in that example. A *blackhead*, on the other hand, is not a kind of head, but a kind of pimple, one that possesses a black head. *Blackhead*, then, is an exocentric compound. In the same way, while a *drawbridge*(吊り上げ橋) is a kind of bridge, a *pickpocket*(スリ(=人)) is not a kind of pocket, but a person who picks pockets: the former verb-noun com-

principled =
法則に基づいた

head = 主要部

Right-hand Head Rule =
右側主要部の規則

endocentric compound =
内心複合語

exocentric compound =
外心複合語

pound is endocentric, while the latter is exocentric. Note that exocentric compounds are not differentiated from endocentric ones by their form, but rather by the fact that they must be interpreted in a special way, in the cases just given either as the possessor of an adjective-noun combination or as the subject of a verb-object combination.

Following the Right-hand Head Rule, more and more complex compounds can be produced. If s*tudent* is added to the compound *high school*, we get a bigger compound, *high school student*. The formation of *high school student* thus involves compounding twice. The result is shown in the **tree diagram** in Figure 1 (CN = compound noun).

tree diagram＝樹形図

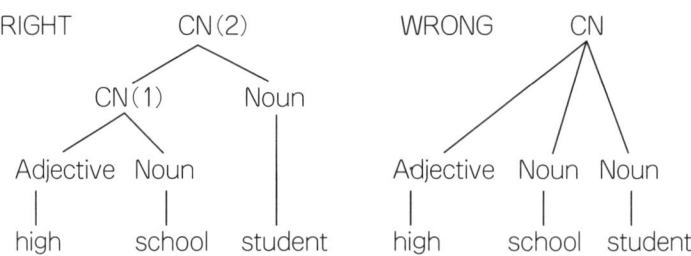

Figure 1 Hierarchical structure   Figure 2 Flat structure

Figure 1 represents the meaning correctly. First, *high* and *school* are combined into the meaning unit CN (1), and then *student* is added to make up the larger unit CN (2). The **hierarchical structure** thus reflects the units of meaning. The fact that the meaning of a complex expression can be built up on the basis of the meanings of its components is referred to as **semantic compositionality**.

hierarchical structure＝階層構造

semantic compositionality＝意味の合成性

Now compare Figure 1 with the "flat" structure in Figure 2. The latter does not show the desired meaning because the three words are simply put together side by side. In fact, there is a general principle of word formation which prohibits combining three or more elements at one time (the **Binary Branching Constraint**). Because of this constraint, large compounds are in principle always made by combining two elements at a time. (Japanese **coordinate compounds** like 松竹梅 constitute an ob-

Binary Branching Constraint＝
二分枝分かれ制約

coordinate compound＝
並列複合語

vious exception.)

It is interesting to note that when several words are combined, different groupings give rise to different meanings. Consider the two meanings of *American football fans*. On one reading, this expression means 'fans of American football'; on the other, it means 'football fans who are Americans'. These two meanings can be represented in different tree diagrams as in (1) and (2), where we omit category names and the internal structure of *football* ((2) is a **noun phrase** rather than a compound noun).

noun phrase = 名詞句

(1) 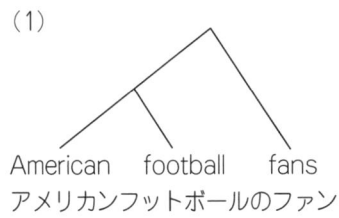   (2)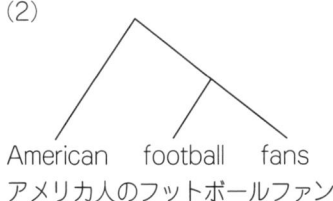

DERIVATION

Derivation is the process of making a word by attaching a bound morpheme to a **base** that may be a word or a bound morpheme. The attached morphemes, called **affixes**, are classified into **prefixes**, which are attached at the beginning of the base, and **suffixes**, which are attached at the end. Each affix places restrictions on the kind of base to which it can attach, particularly with regard to the lexical category of the base. The suffix *-er* (sometimes spelled *-or*) is fairly free, as it can be attached to bases of almost any category: verbs (*singer, actor, computer, refrigerator*), nouns (*New Yorker, teen-ager, double-decker*), adjectives (*foreigner, stranger, Southerner*), and even **numerals** (*fiver*). Most prefixes and suffixes, however, are selective with regard to the category of the base they attach to. The suffix *-ness* attaches only to adjectives, as in *happiness* and *weakness*, refusing nouns (**friendness* vs. *friendliness*), adverbs (**slowliness* vs. *slowness*), and verbs (**attractness* vs. *attractiveness*).

Sometimes an affix that selects two or more different categories seems to vary in meaning depending on the category selected

base = 語基
affix = 接辞
prefix = 接頭辞
suffix = 接尾辞

numeral = 数詞

(it would also be possible to say that in such cases we have two affixes that happen to sound alike). Consider the negative prefix *un-*, which may be attached to adjectives (*unhappy, unkind*) and verbs (*untie, unfasten*) and, very rarely, to nouns (*unemployment, unrest*). When attached to adjectives, *un-* adds a negative meaning to the base, so that *unsafe* means 'not safe' and *uninteresting* means 'not interesting'. But when attached to verbs, *un-* has a different meaning. *Untie* does not mean 'not to tie', nor does *uncover* mean 'not to cover'. Rather, *untie* means 'loosen' and *uncover* means 'remove the cover of'. The *un-* that attaches to verbs, in other words, expresses the reversal of the process expressed by the base verb. This explains why we cannot say **unbelieve* or **unrely*: believing and relying are not reversible. You might immediately point out that *unbelievable* and *unreliable* are nevertheless good English. This is true, but in these words, *un-* is attached not to *believe* and *rely*, as in Figure 3, but rather to the adjectives *believable* and *reliable*, as in Figure 4. The structure of Figure 4 shows correctly that *unbelievable* means 'not believable'.

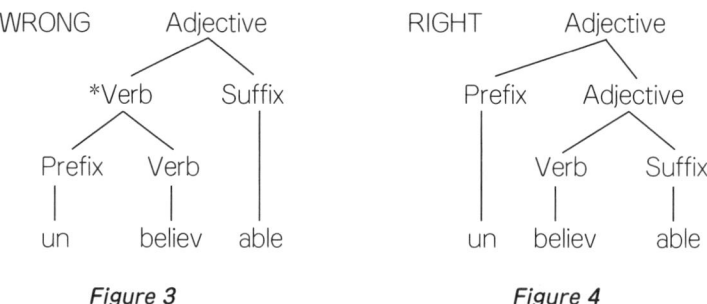

Figure 3   *Figure 4*

CONVERSION

Conversion is the process of changing the category of a word without any alteration of form, and is sometimes regarded as derivation by means of a "zero" (invisible and inaudible) affix. Conversion affects various categories, changing adjectives to verbs (*to warm, to better, to idle*), adjectives to nouns (*a musical, a facial, valuables*), verbs to nouns (*a hit, a look, fries*), and nouns to verbs (*to fax, to bank, to bridge*). Of these, perhaps the most interesting is noun-to-verb conversion, which produces verbs with a wide variety of meanings, as in the following:

1. She *bikes* (*bicycles*) to school.
2. She *buttered* her toast.
3. He had to *shoulder* the responsibility.
4. He *wolfed* down a sandwich and went back to work.
5. Do you *yahoo*?

Despite the wide range of possible meanings, it is not hard to pinpoint the interpretation of a particular **zero-derived** verb in context if we know the meaning of the original noun. Since the noun *bike*, for example, represents something you ride, sentence 1 above is interpreted as meaning 'She rides a bike to school'.

zero-derived = ゼロ派生の

There are also cases of derivation that look like conversion except that they involve changes in vowels and/or consonants. Examples are *shelve* 'to put on a shelf' from *shelf* and *house* [hawz] 'to place in a house' from *house*, in both of which the final consonant of the noun has been **voiced** ([f] becomes [v] and [s] becomes [z]). In *bathe* [beʲð] 'to give a bath' from *bath*, the vowel changes as well as the final consonant.

voice = 有声化する

INFLECTION

Unlike compounding, derivation, and conversion, inflection does not change meaning or category but only adds grammatical information. In English, inflection appears on verbs (past tense *-ed* and third person singular present *-(e)s*), nouns (plural *-(e)s* and **possessive** *-'s*), and adjectives (**comparative** *-er* and **superlative** *-est*). A distinctive property of inflections is that they cannot normally appear inside compounds or **derivatives**; instead, they must appear at the end of such complex words. Compare the unacceptable expressions on the left-hand side with the acceptable ones on the right.

grammatical = 文法上の

possessive = 所有格
comparative = 比較級
superlative = 最上級
derivative = 派生語

*fruits salad	fruit salad
*shoes shop	shoe shop
*arms wrestling	arm wrestling
*happierness, *happiestness	happiness

We can account for the appearance of inflectional material outside of compounds and derivational material by proposing that word formation processes are "ordered" so that inflection takes place after compounding, derivation, and conversion.

> Ordering of word formation processes
> Stage 1: compounding, derivation, conversion
> ↓
> Stage 2: inflection

There are exceptions to the principle that inflected forms cannot appear in compounds, however, as shown by examples like *parks commissioner* 'commissioner of parks', *parts distributor* 'distributor of parts', and *systems analyst* 'analyst of systems'. On the other hand, compounds like *arms control*, *customs inspection*, and *clothes hanger* are only apparent counterexamples to that principle. In such cases, the forms with what looks like plural -s have arguably become words in their own right, sometimes with specialized meanings (*arms* 'weapons'). Such forms, then, are not produced by the operation of inflectional processes, but are remembered by speakers as indivisible units.

MINOR WORD FORMATION PROCESSES

Besides the major types of word formation discussed above, there are a number of minor word formation processes whose operation is typically sporadic—that is, relatively infrequent and irregular.

●**Clipping** (also called **shortening**) is word formation by omission of part of a long word, as in *pro*(fessional), *math*(ematics), *gym*(nasium), *ad*(vertisement), *gas*(oline), *rock*(-'n'-roll), and *fax* (from *facsimile*).

●**Blending** is the combination of parts of two different words. Typical English examples are *smog* from *sm*(oke) + (f)*og*, *brunch* from *br*(eakfast) + (l)*unch*, *motel* from *mo*(tor) + (ho)*tel*, and

---

ordered = 順序付けられている

arguably = ほぼ間違いなく

clipping = 短縮
shortening = 短縮

blending = 混成

heliport from *heli*(copter) + (air)*port*. Note that all of these examples combine the beginning of the first word and the end of the second. A kind of blending that combines the beginnings of two words is extremely common and regular in colloquial Japanese, as in the examples デジカメ from デジ(タル)＋カメ(ラ) and ジーパン from ジー(ンズ)＋パン(ツ).

●In an **acronym**, the first letters of several words are combined into a new word in which each letter is pronounced with its ordinary **phonetic** value. Examples are *laser* from "*l*ight *a*mplification by *s*timulated *e*mission of *r*adiation," *scuba*(diving) from "*s*elf-*c*ontained *u*nderwater *b*reathing *a*pparatus," and *NASA* from "*N*ational *A*eronautics and *S*pace *A*dministration." Words formed from initial letters in which each letter is pronounced as its conventional name([ej] for *a*, [bij] for *b*, etc.) are sometimes grouped together with acronyms, but are more properly called **initialisms**. Typical examples, the first two very recent in origin, are *IT*(information technology), *ATM*(automated/automatic teller machine), and *DNA*(deoxyribonucleic acid). Sometimes the pronunciation of a word varies between that appropriate to an acronym and that appropriate to an initialism. Thus *UFO*(unidentified flying object) is known to one of the authors of this book only in the "initialism" form [juw ef ow], but is listed in some dictionaries in the "acronym" form [juwfow].

acronym＝頭文字語

phonetic＝音声的な

initialism＝頭文字表記語

逆形成

　ふつう，小さい単語から大きな単語が出来るが，逆に，大きな単語が小さくなる場合もある。本文で挙げた短縮，混成，頭文字語がそれに当たるが，これらは，単に発音や綴りを切りつめるだけで，品詞の変更などの文法的な働きはない。これに対して，windowshopping という複合名詞から windowshop という複合動詞を作るような例がある。windowshopping は，もともと window と shopping を複合したものだが，その中の -ing を取り外して，windowshop という動詞ができている。外見上は，名詞(window)＋動詞(shop)の組み合わせのように見えるが，英語では，ふつう，名詞と動詞を直接に複合することはできない。このように，規則的な語形成によるのではなく，勝手に単語の語尾を削り取って別の品詞の単語に変えることを逆形成(backformation)という。類似の例には，editor(編集者)から edit(編集する)，air-conditioner から air-condition，freeze-drying から freeze-dry(凍結乾燥させる)などがある。

Comprehension Check

✎ 空所を埋めなさい。

単語の構造を研究する分野を（　　　）といい，意味のある最も小さい要素を（　　　）と呼ぶ。これには，単独で語として使える（　　　）と，それだけでは単語として独立しない（　　　）の2種類がある。英語で単語を作る主要な方法は（　　　），（　　　），（　　　），（　　　）の4つである。（　　　）は単語を2つずつ組み合わせていくやり方であり，（　　　）は語基(base)の前に（　　　）を付けたり，後ろに（　　　）を付けたりする方法である。（　　　）は単語の形はそのままで（あるいはゼロの接辞を付けて），（　　　）を変える方法で，これには，a weekly のように（　　　）から（　　　）を作ったり，butter the toast のように（　　　）から（　　　）を作ったりといろいろなケースがある。（　　　）は，動詞なら（　　　）を表す語尾，名詞なら（　　　）を表す語尾，形容詞なら（　　　）と最上級の語尾のように，文法的情報を付け加える働きをする。

Exercises

(1) 各組の単語に共通する形態素を抜き出し，その意味を説明しなさい。

　　a. octopus, October, octave, octagon, octet
　　b. morphology, biology, archaeology, geology, Japanology
　　c. portable, export, transportation, support, report

(2) 例にならって，複合語に書き換えなさい。また，複合語に書き換えたときに順番が入れ替わるのはなぜか説明しなさい。

　　[例] He drives a taxi. → He is a (taxi) (driver).
　　a. a student in history → a (　　　) (　　　)
　　b. This computer is friendly to users. → This computer is (　　　)-(　　　).
　　c. The pianist is famous throughout the world. → She is a (　　　)-(　　　) pianist.
　　d. He won the prize at the contest. → He was the (　　　)-(　　　) at the contest.

(3) 複合語（左側）と句（右側）で第一強勢のあるところにアクセントの印(´)をつけ，各々の意味を述べなさい。

	複合語	句
a.	blueberries	the blue sky

b. a kickoff　　　　　　　　(They) kicked off.
c. sleeping pills　　　　　　a sleeping baby
d. softball　　　　　　　　 a soft ball

(4) 次の複合語で第一強勢のあるところにアクセントの印(´)をつけ，「複合語強勢規則」に従うものと従わないものとの違いを検討しなさい。

  a. hardware　　b. hard-boiled　　c. hard copy
  d. hard-hitting　e. hard-pressed　　f. hard disk

(5) 示された順序にしたがって，枝分かれ構造（樹形図）を組み立てなさい。出来上がった結果が，右側主要部の規則に合っているかどうか，検討しなさい。

  a. educate→接尾辞 -ion を付ける→接尾辞 -al を付ける
  b. fortune→接尾辞 -ate を付ける→接頭辞 un- を付ける→接尾辞 -ly を付ける
  c. pass→接尾辞 -er を付ける→その後ろに小辞(particle)の by を複合する

(6) 次の複合語ないし派生語の意味を述べ，その形態構造を樹形図で示しなさい。特に d は，2 通りの意味があるので，それぞれの意味に応じて 2 つの構造を示す。

  a. baseball player
  b. Japan Olympic Committee chairman
  c. unreliableness [ヒント：un- は形容詞に付き，-ness は形容詞に付く。]
  d. unlockable [ヒント：lock は動詞。]

(7) 次の語の形成過程を説明しなさい（複数の語形成過程が関わる場合もある）。

  a. Internet　　　b. fridge　　　　　c. loveliest
  d. weaknesses　e. whale-watching　f. astrology
  g. PTA　　　　 h. PET (bottle)　　i. She <u>sugared</u> her coffee.

Chapter 4 How Words Mean: Semantics I

> **BASIC QUESTIONS**
> 単語の意味が分からないときは辞書をひくが,「意味」というのは一体,何だろう。
> 辞書は 1 つ 1 つの単語の意味を別々に載せているだけだが,ネイティヴスピーカーが何千,何万の単語を使いこなせるのは,単語が互いに何らかの意味のつながりを持っているからではないだろうか。

What's in a name? That which we call a rose
By any other name would smell as sweet.

— William Shakespeare, *Romeo and Juliet*, II.ii.

でも,名前が一体なんだろう? 私たちがバラと呼んでいるあの花の名前がなんと変わろうとも,薫りに違いはないはずよ。

(中野好夫 訳)

KINDS OF MEANING

When we come across a word we don't understand, we look it up in a dictionary. But what a dictionary shows us is not really the meaning of the word but merely a "translation" or roundabout explanation. The real meanings of words are concepts stored in our mind. The study of the **meaning** of words and sentences is called semantics, and this chapter will examine the meanings of words.

There are two kinds of word meaning: **conceptual meaning** (or **denotation**) and **associative meaning** (or **connotation**). The conceptual meaning of the word *rose* is 'plant of the rose family (the genus *Rosa*)'. But that is not all there is to roses. We have all seen, smelled, and touched actual roses (that is, **referents** of the word *rose*) at various times and places. Those experiences as well as cultural traditions have formed our subjective images of roses, which include elements such as their appearance and smell. Some of those images of roses are associated with the linguistic meaning of the word *rose*. Such associative meanings often show up in proverbs ("Life is not a bed of *roses*") and idioms.

conceptual meaning = 概念的意味
denotation = 明示的意味
associative meaning = 連想的意味
connotation = 暗示的意味
referent = 指示対象

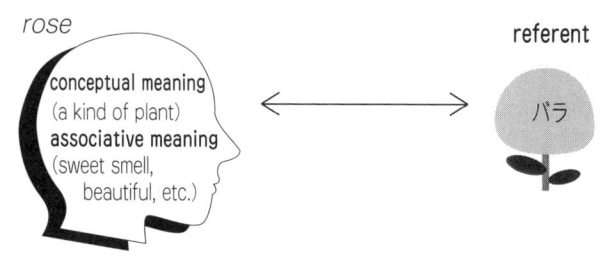

Figure 1 Relationship between meaning and referent

MEANING AS A SET OF PROPERTIES

The full meaning of a word is a **set** of conceptual and associative meanings. Those meanings are defined in terms of **entailment** relations. We say "X entails Y" if Y necessarily follows from X. Consider, for example, the verb *drown*, which is defined in dictionaries as 'to die in water because one is unable to breathe'. Upon hearing the sentence *The boy drowned in the river*, we necessarily understand that the boy died. It is thus a **contradiction** to say **The boy drowned in the river, but he didn't die.* (Here, the asterisk(*) shows that the expression is semantically odd though grammatically fine.) Note that the opposite is not always the case; even if you say *The boy died,* it does not follow that he drowned.

- *The boy drowned* **entails** *The boy died.*
- *The boy died* does not entail *The boy drowned.*

We assume that a meaning which is entailed by a word is included in its conceptual meaning. Thus, *drown* contains the meaning of 'dying', but *die* does not contain the meaning of 'drowning'.

The entailment relation holds for nouns as well. If you grow roses in the garden, then it necessarily follows that you grow plants. Being a rose entails being a plant (*This is a rose, so it is a plant*). Let us try this out with the noun *bus*.

(1) This is a bus, so it is {a vehicle / *furniture}.
(2) This is a bus, so it is supposed to {carry passengers / *carry goods and materials}.
(3) This is a bus, so it is supposed to {run according to a schedule / *come at your request}.

(1) shows that a bus is a vehicle, not furniture. (2) and (3) show that a bus has the function of carrying people according to a schedule. If we try the same test with the nouns *taxi* and *truck*, we will be able to capture the similarities and differences between them, as in Table 1.

---

set＝集合
entailment＝（論理的）含意
Y follows from X＝
X の当然の結果として Y になる

contradiction＝矛盾

entail＝含意する

it follows that〜＝
当然〜ということになる

	(1) a kind of vehicle	(2) intended to carry people	(3) supposed to run according to a schedule
bus	+	+	+
taxi	+	+	−
truck	+	−	−

Table 1 Similarities and differences between words

Here, the three words have in common the feature [vehicle], a feature whose meaning is 'a means of transporting passengers or goods'.

feature＝素性，特徴

CATEGORIZATION AND PROTOTYPES

Words are names that help us **categorize** the things around us. The feature [vehicle] groups together buses, taxis, trucks, trains, boats, airplanes, hovercrafts, and many other things that have, broadly, the same function. More generally, if we come across an object that we are not acquainted with, we categorize it first according to whether it is a living thing or not, and then, if it is living, according to whether it is a mammal, bird, reptile, or fish, etc., and if it is not living, according to what purposes it is used for.

categorize＝類別する（カテゴリー化する）

Such mental processes of **categorization** make up word meanings, and the word meanings in turn determine, to a large extent, the way the native speakers understand the world around them (**The Sapir-Whorf Hypothesis**). A classic example involves expressions related to food. What is referred to by the single word *rice* in English is categorized in Japanese into several notions (稲, 米, and 飯 or ご飯) depending on the state and function of the grain. Conversely, what is referred to by the single word 羊 in Japanese is divided in English into *sheep, ram, ewe, lamb,* and *mutton* (meat), depending on sex, age, and function. Lexical distinctions of this kind can be seen as reflecting the culture of a particular linguistic community. However, the fact that a language lacks a lexical distinction does not mean that the speakers of that language are incapable of perceiving or understanding the distinction. English has a lot of names for hair colors such as *blonde, brunet, auburn,* and *flaxen*. Although

categorization＝類別化，カテゴリー化

Sapir-Whorf Hypothesis＝サピア・ウォーフの仮説

lexical＝語彙の

Japanese doesn't have corresponding terms, speakers of Japanese can certainly perceive the differences in question.

With associative meanings, entailment relations do not always give a clear-cut result. If you say *This is a rose*, it follows that it is a plant, but it does not necessarily follow that it is fragrant or has red petals. Those things are typical of roses but are not shared by all examples, or tokens, of the category. **Tokens** that have all the typical characteristics of a category are **prototypical** examples of that category, and represent its **prototype**. Shakespeare's famous passage quoted at the beginning of the chapter takes advantage of one of the prototypical properties of roses. Let us take birds as another example. Typically, birds have wings and feathers, fly in the sky, have beaks, lay eggs, and so on. Robins and sparrows have all these characteristics and are therefore prototypical examples of birds. On the other hand, penguins, ostriches, kiwis, and chickens are not prototypical birds because they lack one or more of the properties that define the bird prototype.

token＝具体的な使用例
prototypical＝原型的
prototype＝
原型，プロトタイプ

SEMANTIC NETWORKS

Words are related to each other in a way that can be represented by **semantic networks**. A semantic network is a group of words with similar meanings organized into a hierarchical structure based on **hyponymy** relations.

semantic network＝
意味のネットワーク

hyponymy＝
上下関係(包摂関係とも言う)

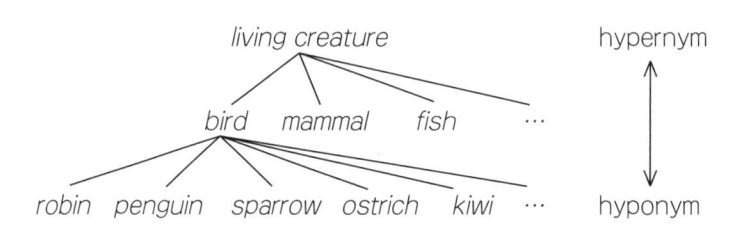

Figure 2 The relation of hyponymy

Hyponymy is a "kind-of" relation. A bird is a kind of animal, and a penguin is a kind of bird. The hierarchy goes further down as you add more and more specific names. A more general (higher) term is called a **hypernym**, and a more specific (lower) term a **hyponym**.

hypernym＝上位語
hyponym＝下位語

Hyponymy should not be mixed up with **meronymy**, which is a "part-whole" relation. For example, *house* represents a whole, of which *roof, wall, room, entrance,* and other things are parts.

meronymy＝部分関係

Verbs also form semantic networks. Consider how English verbs of laughing and smiling are related to each other. In Figure 3, note that English lacks a general term which, like Japanese 笑う, covers both sounds (laughing) and facial expressions (smiling).

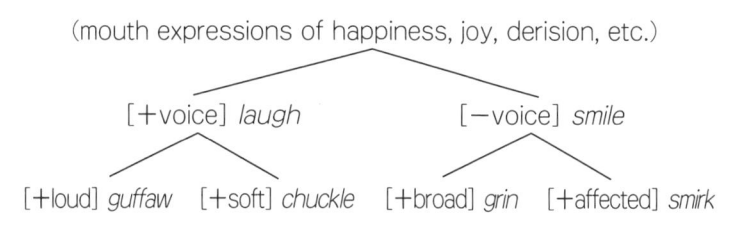

(mouth expressions of happiness, joy, derision, etc.)

[＋voice] *laugh*   [−voice] *smile*

[＋loud] *guffaw*   [＋soft] *chuckle*   [＋broad] *grin*   [＋affected] *smirk*

Figure 3 Verbs of laughing and smiling

The semantic relations among words can be more complex than the simple hierarchies in Figures 2 and 3, because the defining features of categories may cut across each other. Figure 4 shows how various names of vehicles are related to each other.

vehicle

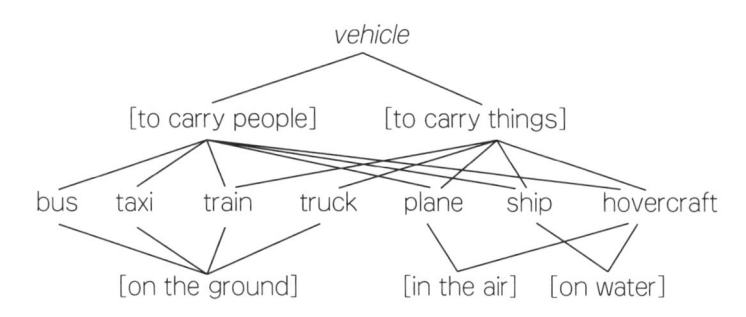

[to carry people]   [to carry things]

bus   taxi   train   truck   plane   ship   hovercraft

[on the ground]   [in the air]   [on water]

Figure 4 Vehicle terms

SYNONYMS AND ANTONYMS

While hyponymy and hypernymy are "vertical" relationships among semantically related words, **synonymy** and **antonymy** refer to special cases of the "horizontal" relationships in a hierarchy.

synonymy＝同義関係
antonymy＝反義関係

Synonymy is the well-known semantic relation that holds

between two or more words having the same meaning. It is often said, however, that no two words are exact **synonyms**. Even if the conceptual meanings are identical, associative meanings or usage may differ. *Fall* and *autumn, father* and *dad, buy* and *purchase* are often regarded as synonymous but are different in style or connotation, as well as in some cases being characteristic of different regional dialects.

The opposition of meanings is called antonymy. There are at least two different kinds. Consider adjectives like *big* and *small, rich* and *poor*, or *quiet* and *noisy*. Whether something is big or small is a matter of degree, so you can deny both (*This is neither too big nor too small*) or emphasize or compare the degree to which the adjective is applicable (*He is very big / He is bigger than his brother*). These **gradable antonyms** contrast with **non-gradable** ones like *dead* and *alive, male* and *female*, or *heads* and *tails*. These are either-or choices that allow no intermediate degrees. It is not normal to say **He is neither dead nor alive,* nor is it possible to express degree with such words (**He is very dead / *He is more dead than his brother*).

POLYSEMY

So far we have assumed that a given word has only one meaning. In actuality, however, many words are **ambiguous** and can be interpreted in two or more different ways. If someone just says, "This food is hot," it is not clear whether he means the food is heated or spicy. Although 熱い and 辛い in Japanese are distinct concepts, the two meanings of the English *hot* are originally the same, the 'spicy' sense being derived from the 'high temperature' sense through the burning sensation in the mouth. If a word has two or more meanings that are related to each other in some way or other, the word is said to be **polysemous**.

Polysemy should be distinguished from **homonymy**, in which two or more words that have no semantic connection happen to be pronounced (or spelled) in the same way. Common examples are *bat* in baseball and *bat* as a flying mammal, or the noun *bear* and the verb *bear*.

METAPHOR AND METONYMY

A problem in semantics is how polysemy comes about. How does the word *down* represent three different but related meanings in *The stock market went down, I feel down today,* and *My computer is down*? We can say the various meanings are extended from the physical sense of *down* by way of **metaphor**. Metaphor is a way of describing one thing in terms of another thing that belongs to a different semantic area. The spatial concept "down" is compared to the low level of prices, the subject's depressed feeling, and the disabled state of the computer. Similarly, in *She was the rose of the party*, her conspicuous figure at the party is captured by a metaphor from the world of plants, where roses stand out among other flowers.

metaphor = メタファー (隠喩)

Another cause of polysemy is **metonymy**, in which the name of one object is used to refer to another object with which it has a part-whole relationship or other close association. Consider the different meanings of *New York* in *He went to New York* (the city) and *New York has just elected a new mayor* (people of that city). The name of a city ("whole") represents the people living there ("part"). Similarly, *the bottle* in *She broke the bottle* refers to the container, whereas the same word in *She finished the bottle* means the contents of the container. In a case like *These lands belong to the crown*, the term *crown* is used to refer to the monarchy or the royal family, items with which a crown is naturally associated. Metaphor and metonymy, which are often thought of as rhetorical techniques of literature, are actually an integral part of the daily use of words. They are certainly among the basic human abilities that help us enlarge the scope of our perception and conceptualization. It should be noted, however, that although these mechanisms appear to be universal in human language, the way they work in individual words and phrases may differ from

metonymy = メトニミー (換喩)

rhetorical = 修辞的な

perception = 知覚
conceptualization = 概念化
universal = 普遍的な

language to language. For example, the "UP-DOWN metaphor," pointed out by the linguist George Lakoff, is widespread in both English and Japanese.

MORE IS UP; LESS IS DOWN.
Our income rose last year.　去年は給料が上がった。
Their income fell this year.　今年は給料が下がった。

HAPPY IS UP; SAD IS DOWN.
Our spirits rose.　　　　　　意気が上がった。
His spirits fell at the news.　ニュースを聞いて気分が落ち込んだ。

In these examples, the original meaning of physical motion is extended to an abstract change of state.

A parallel **extension** of meaning is common with English *go* and *come*: when combined with adjectives, *go* generally means a change into a bad or unfavorable condition, and *come* generally means a change into a good or favorable condition. This is illustrated by the following examples:

extension＝拡張

The milk went sour.　　*ミルクが酸味に行った。
　　　　　　　　　　　（ミルクがすっぱくなった）

His dream came true.　*彼の夢は現実に来た。
　　　　　　　　　　　（夢が現実になった）

In this case, however, direct translations into Japanese are unacceptable. The semantic extension that occurs quite commonly with *go* and *come* does not apply to Japanese 行く and 来る.

Comprehension Check

✎ 空所を埋めなさい。

ことばの意味を研究する分野を(　　　)という。意味には，大きく分けて2種類ある。たとえば，rose という名詞が「バラ科の植物」を表すというのは(　　　)的意味であり，「香しい臭いがする」とか「きれいだ」とかいったイメージは(　　　)的意味である。単語と単語の意味の類似性を表す関係には，deep と profound のような(　　　)，fish と salmon のような(　　　)，car と tire のような(　　　)がある。逆に，意味が反対であることを表す関係は(　　　)であるが，それは，細かく見れば，rich 対 poor のような(　　　)と，boy 対 girl のような(　　　)に分かれる。たまたま発音が同じだけで，意味は全然ちがうという関係は(　　　)という。多くの場合，1つの単語には複数の意味が関わっている。このことを(　　　)という。基本的な意味が他の関連する意味に拡張していくのは，(　　　)や(　　　)などのメカニズムに依る。

Exercises

(1) 左側の文が右側の文を「含意」する関係が成り立つかどうか判断しなさい。

a. The boy ate an orange. → The boy ate some fruit.
b. The boy ate some fruit. → The boy ate an orange.
c. The policeman shot at the criminal. → The bullet hit the criminal.
d. The policeman shot the criminal. → The bullet hit the criminal.
e. I dropped the plate. → The plate broke.
f. I smashed the plate. → The plate broke into pieces.

(2) 下線部の単語がどのような連想的意味を表現するか説明しなさい。

a. He is a green, insecure accountant from New Jersey on a once-a-year trip to the West Coast.
b. I'm not exactly a spring chicken any more, dear.
c. Why do you keep that old car? It's a real lemon.
d. That is a {womanish / womanly} attitude.

(3) 次は，at, on, in, to, onto, into, from, off, out of という9つの前置詞の意味を意味成分で分析した表である。空欄に適切な前置詞を当てはめなさい。

	一点	表面	内部
そこに接触した静止状態			
そこへの移動			
そこからの移動			
そこから離れた静止状態			

(4) 次は類義語間の意味のネットワークを示している。適切な単語を下から選んで空所に入れなさい。

a. 歩行の動詞　《stagger, pace, trudge, limp, tiptoe, toddle》

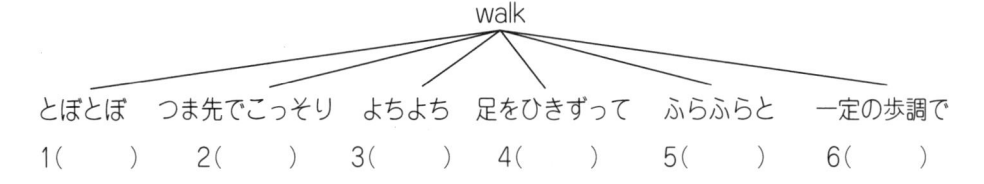

```
                        walk
   ┌──────┬──────┬──────┬──────┬──────┐
 とぼとぼ つま先でこっそり よちよち 足をひきずって ふらふらと 一定の歩調で
 1(   )  2(   )   3(   )  4(   )     5(   )   6(   )
```

b. 調理の動詞　《simmer, barbecue, boil, deep-fry, fry, sauté, grill, stew》

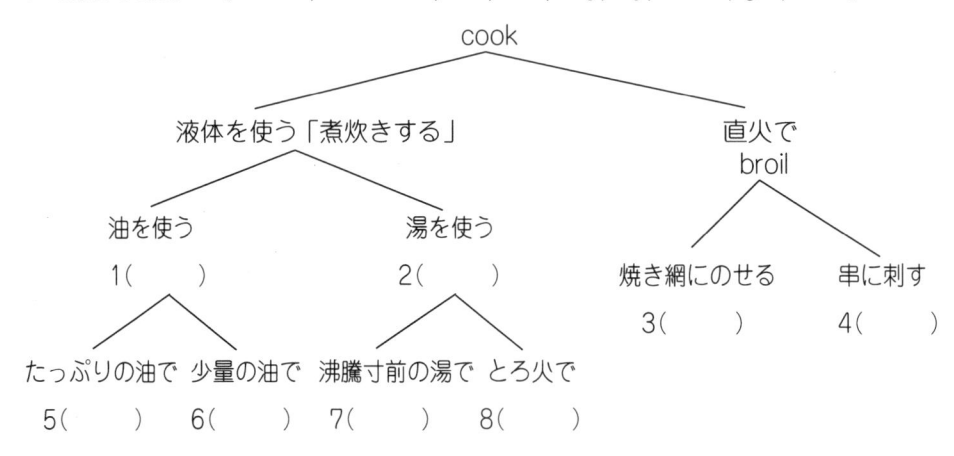

```
                       cook
         ┌──────────────────┴──────────────┐
     液体を使う「煮炊きする」                直火で
                                            broil
      ┌──────┴──────┐                 ┌──────┴──────┐
    油を使う       湯を使う         焼き網にのせる   串に刺す
    1(   )         2(   )            3(   )        4(   )
   ┌──┴──┐      ┌──┴──┐
たっぷりの油で 少量の油で 沸騰寸前の湯で とろ火で
 5(   )    6(   )    7(   )     8(   )
```

(5) 各組の単語の意味関係に該当する専門用語を下から選びなさい。

《同義関係, 段階的反義関係, 非段階的反義関係, 同音異義, 上下関係, 部分関係, 多義性》

a. shoe / sole　　　b. dull / sharp　　　c. asleep / awake
d. poodle / dog　　e. shop / store　　　f. bark (of a tree) / bark (of a dog)
g. fair ball / foul ball　h. clock / watch　i. garbage can / dustbin
j. book / cover　　k. star (in the sky) / star (in the movie)

(6) メタファーは，具体的，物理的なものを土台 (source) として，抽象的な観念をそれにたとえることが多い。次の各組で，メタファーの土台となるのは a か b か？また，その土台のどのような意味的性質がメタファーに利用されているか述べなさい。

1. a. This bottle is narrow at the <u>mouth</u>.
   b. He is sleeping with his <u>mouth</u> open.
2. a. He used a <u>ladder</u> to get to the roof.
   b. He began his career from the bottom of the <u>ladder</u>.
3. a. He <u>fell</u> silent.
   b. He <u>fell</u> into a manhole.
4. a. He lives <u>over</u> the mountain.
   b. He is <u>over</u> his cold.
5. a. Hi! What's <u>up</u>?
   b. The curtain is <u>up</u> and the play has begun.

(7) hand という名詞は，文字通りの「手」のほかに，いろいろな意味がある。次の hand の多義性がメタファーによるものかメトニミーによるものか考えなさい。

a. This bag is very heavy. Will you give me a <u>hand</u>?
b. I want to buy a watch with a second <u>hand</u>.
c. Please give the players a big <u>hand</u>.
d. The book was translated by various <u>hands</u>.

コトバの価値判断

　　big と small は反義語であるが，この2つは対等ではない。一般的に，人間は小さいより大きい方が良いと判断する。そのため，人にものを尋ねる場合も，How big is your house? （お宅は，どれほどの大きさですか）と言うのが普通であり，*How small is your house? と言うのは，大変失礼になる。身長を尋ねるのに，How tall are you? と言って，*How short are you? と言わないのも，そのためである。これはしかし，礼儀の問題ではない。small に対して big は肯定的，short に対して tall は肯定的である。short に対する long, shallow に対する deep, near に対する far, little に対する much, few に対する many もそうである。このように，ペアになっている反義語を使って How ～? と尋ねる場合は，プラスと評価される方の単語を使う。true or false, right or wrong, life and death のように反対語を2つ並べるときも，肯定的なものが先に来ることが多い（ただし，life and death が形容詞になると，dead or alive のように，発音上，長いほうが後ろに来る）。right（正しい）という単語が「右の」という意味を持つのも，人間は右利きのほうが多く，右手のほうが左手より力が強くて重要だという判断と関係している。

Chapter 5 How English Phrases Are Formed: Syntax I

> **BASIC QUESTIONS**
> 第 3 章では単語の作り方を学んだが，単語はどのように句(phrase)に組み合わせられるのだろうか。高校の英文法では SVO などの五文型を学んだが，S(主語)，V(動詞)，O(目的語)はこの順序で一列に並んでいるだけなのだろうか。

WHAT IS SYNTAX?

While morphology, as we saw in Chapter 3, deals with how words are formed, syntax is concerned with the way words are combined to make phrases and sentences. One of the most fundamental facts about the grammar of any human language is that the words of a sentence are not simply lined up one after the other, but are organized into **syntactic** units, or **constituents**. Thus, for example, the way the SVO (subject verb object) sentence pattern is taught in high school might suggest that the three elements involved are strung together and organized into a single group as in (1) below.

syntactic = 統語的な，構文上の
unit = まとまり，単位
constituent = 構成素

(1)
```
        Sentence
       /   |    \
  Subject Verb Object
```

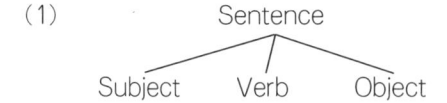

As we will see below, however, there are many reasons to believe that these three elements are actually organized in a hierarchical structure like (2). The structure in (2) differs from (1) in including a syntactic unit called **verb phrase** that consists of V and O to the exclusion of S.

verb phrase (VP) = 動詞句

(2)
```
        Sentence
       /        \
  Subject    Verb Phrase
              /     \
           Verb    Object
```

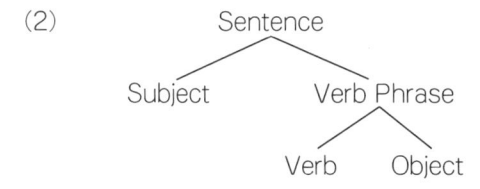

One way to appreciate the existence of syntactic constituents is to consider the ambiguity (double meaning) of a phrase like (3), whose two interpretations are given in (4).

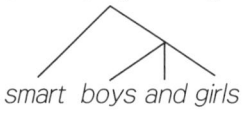

(3) smart boys and girls
(4) a. boys who are smart and girls who are smart
    b. boys who are smart and (all) girls

It is natural to see the two interpretations of (4), respectively, as the result of two alternative groupings of the words of (3), namely those in (5).

(5) a. [smart [boys and girls]]   b. [[smart boys] and girls]

    smart boys and girls   smart boys and girls

Depending on how the words of (3) are organized into constituents, in other words, the interpretation of the whole phrase will differ.

TESTS FOR CONSTITUENCY

argument＝論拠，理由

The argument for grouping of words into constituents that we applied above to example (3) is essentially a semantic argument, or one concerned with meaning. In this section, we will look briefly at four syntactic tests that can distinguish when a sequence of words forms a constituent. As an example of a constituent, we use the verb phrase (VP), which consists of a verb (V) along with its objects and **modifiers**, if any. The "syntactic unit that consists of V and O to the exclusion of S" that we showed in (2) is precisely a VP.

modifier＝修飾語

movement＝移動

Test 1: Movement

string of words＝
単語の連鎖

A **string of words** is a constituent if it can be moved or displaced as a unit from its expected location. Consider in this regard example (6), which includes a moved VP that has been underlined:

(6) Jim said that Sue would refuse the offer, and <u>refuse the offer</u> she did.

criterion＝基準

The expected location for a VP in English (and most other languages as well) is after the subject that corresponds to it. By that criterion, the second occurrence of the VP *refuse the offer* in (6) is not in its expected location, since it precedes the corresponding subject *she* (we would, that is, expect the word order *she did refuse the offer*). The second VP in (6) has evidently been moved from its expected location to pre-subject position. Crucially, it is not possible to move just the V, leaving the object behind:

pre-subject position＝
主語より前の位置

(7) *Jim said that Sue would refuse the offer, and <u>refuse</u> she did <u>the offer</u>.

Test 2: Deletion

A string of words is a constituent if it can be deleted (omitted or removed) from its expected location as a unit. In examples (8), the material that is crossed out can be deleted without affecting the meaning of the sentence.

deletion＝削除

delete＝消す，削除する
omit＝省略する

(8) a. Sue will refuse the offer, and Jim will ~~refuse the offer~~ too.
    b. Sue will refuse the offer, but Jim won't ~~refuse the offer~~.

Here again, it is not possible to delete just the verb, leaving the object behind:

(9) *Sue will refuse the offer, and Jim will ~~refuse~~ the offer too.

What is being deleted in (8), then, is a VP. In Chapter 6, we will look more closely at this process of **VP-deletion**.

VP-deletion＝動詞句削除

Test 3: Pro-forms

A string of words is a constituent if it can serve as the **antecedent** for a word that is interpreted as if it were a copy of that antecedent; such words are called **pro-forms**. The classic case of a proform is a pronoun — for example, the *he* of *The boy left, but **he** came right back,* where *he* is understood to refer to the same person as *the boy*. Example (10) contains a pro-VP *so* whose antecedent is underlined:

antecedent＝先行詞

pro-form＝代用形

refer to＝〜を指す
pro-VP＝VPの代用形

(10) Sue will <u>refuse the offer</u>, and so will Jim.

Note that it is not possible to interpret *so* as referring to just the V in (10) (nor is there another pro-form that allows this):

(11) *Sue will <u>refuse</u> the offer, and so will Jim the offer.

Test 4: Coordination

A string of words is a constituent if it and a parallel but distinct string can occur in the **coordinate structure** frame *both* ___ *and* ___ or *either* ___ *or* ___, as with the VPs of (12) (underlined):

(12) Sue will both <u>refuse the offer</u> and <u>decline the invitation</u>.

COMPLEMENTS AND ADJUNCTS

We have just considered a number of tests showing that VP is a constituent, where we defined VP as "a verb along with its objects and modifiers, if any." Let us think a little more about the distinction between objects and modifiers — alternatively, the distinction between **complements** and **adjuncts**, where "complement" is a more general and abstract version of "object" and "adjunct" a more general and abstract version of "modifier." The verb (V) of a VP, first of all, is the central element, or **head**, of that VP, where the head of a phrase can be defined as the element within it that determines the properties of the phrase as a whole. In the VP *drinking tea*, for example (as in *He is drinking tea*), one way we know that the V *drinking* is the head is that *drinking tea* expresses a "kind" of drinking (and not, for example, a kind of tea).

The complement of a head is the phrase which has the closest possible relationship to the head. Complements include not only the direct and indirect objects of **transitive verbs**, but also the **prepositional phrases** of combinations like *look <u>at the picture</u>* and *depend <u>on the teacher</u>*. We have seen that a verb and its object form a constituent (VP) that excludes the subject, so a subject is clearly not a complement. The same is true of an adjunct, which is an optional element that expresses an adverbial meaning, typically instrument, manner, time, place, or reason. In *Jim ate his dinner with his fingers in his room, his dinner* is a complement, but *with his fingers* and *in his room* are adjuncts. That the complement has a closer relationship with the verb than an adjunct in such a case can be shown by displaying a "pro-form" whose antecedent must include a complement, but can exclude an adjunct. The pro-form *do so* has these properties, as can be seen from the examples of (13), where underlines identify *do so*'s antecedent.

(13) a. Jim <u>ate a cookie</u>, and Sue did so too.
b. *Jim <u>ate</u> a cookie, and Sue did so a cracker.
c. Jim <u>ate</u> with a spoon, and Sue did so with a fork.

While the distinction between a head and a phrase based on it is a fundamental one, there are nevertheless phrases that consist of nothing but a head — phrases, that is, whose head has no complements or modifiers. Thus *refused* in (14a) functions in the same way — as the predicate of the sentence — as does *politely refused the offer* in (14b). The former, like the latter, therefore constitutes a VP even though it is a bare verb with no complement or modifier:

bare＝はだかの

(14) a. Sue <u>refused</u>.
b. Sue <u>politely refused the offer</u>.

CROSS-CATEGORIAL PARALLELISM

We have been looking at VPs headed by the V *refuse*. **Noun phrases**(NPs) **headed by** the related noun *refusal* are fundamentally parallel in structure, as suggested by a comparison of (15) below with (14):

cross-categorial parallelism＝異なる範疇にまたがる並行性
noun phrase(NP)＝名詞句
headed by～＝
～を主要部とする

(15) a. Sue's <u>refusal</u> (cf. 14a)
b. Sue's <u>polite refusal of the offer</u> (cf. 14b)

In particular, NPs, like VPs, may contain complements and adjuncts in addition to a head, and may be combined with a "subject"(*Sue* in (14), *Sue's* in (15)). **Adjective phrases**(APs) and prepositional phrases(PPs), like VPs and NPs, may include complements and adjuncts. Thus, just as (16a) below is a VP headed by *refuse* and (16b) is an NP headed by *refusal*, (16c) is

adjective phrase(AP)＝形容詞句

an AP headed by *proud*, and (16d) is a PP headed by *in*.

(16) a. [politely [**refused** the offer]]
b. [polite [**refusal** of the offer]]
c. [very [**proud** of his son]]
d. [right [**in** the house]]

bracket = 角括弧

In each example of (16), the inner brackets enclose the head-complement combination, and the outer brackets enclose the entire phrase. Those brackets thus express the claim that the head-complement combination forms a constituent that excludes the adjunct.

LABELED BRACKETINGS AND TREE DIAGRAMS

The brackets of (16) express no information about what kind of constituents they enclose and are in that sense incomplete. It is possible to add labels to brackets to supply this information. Consider as an example the VP *meet the man with the binoculars* (binoculars = 双眼鏡). In that VP, the string of words *with the binoculars* is a prepositional modifier on the NP *the man*, and the combination *the man with the binoculars*, which can be paraphrased "the man who has the binoculars," also constitutes an NP. The structure of the whole VP can thus be (roughly) represented as the **labeled bracketing** (17):

paraphrase = 言い換える

labeled bracketing = 標示付き括弧づけ

(17) [$_{VP}$ meet [$_{NP}$ [$_{NP}$ the man] [$_{PP}$ with the binoculars]]]

tree diagram = 樹形図, 枝分かれ図
node = 節点

There is another way, however, often easier to understand, of representing the information shown in (17). This is a **tree diagram**, which displays the structure of a phrase as a set of **nodes** or points, each representing a constituent, that are connected by lines showing how smaller constituents are combined into larger ones (we have in fact already seen rudimentary tree diagrams in (5) above). The node representing the entire phrase under consideration is typically shown at the top of the diagram. Thus, for example, the information shown by the labeled bracketing (17) can also be represented in the form of the tree diagram (18) (as is customary, we use triangles for phrases whose internal structure is not displayed):

(18)
```
        VP
       /  \
      V    NP
     meet / \
         NP  PP
          △   △
      the man with the
              binoculars
```

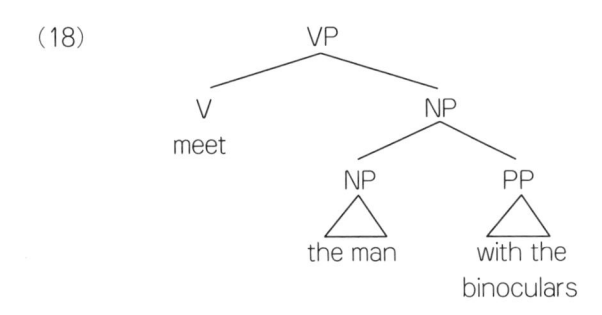

(18)では，with the binoculars は the man という NP を修飾している。

Something interesting happens if we replace the verb *meet* in example (18) with *watch*. The VP *watch the man with the binoculars* is ambiguous in a way that the VP of (17) and (18) is not — that is, it has two distinct interpretations, much as was the case with (3) above. In particular, the PP *with the binoculars* can be interpreted not only as a modifier of the NP *the man*, as in (17) and (18), but also as a modifier of the VP *watch the man*; in this case, the entire VP can be paraphrased "watch the man using the binoculars." Crucially, this ambiguity can be represented as an ambiguity of constituent structure as shown by a labeled bracketing or a tree diagram. Thus, while on one interpretation, *watch the man with the binoculars* will have a structure completely parallel to that shown in (17) and (18), on the other interpretation, it will have the structure shown in (19) and (20) below:

(19) [$_{VP}$ [$_{VP}$ watch [$_{NP}$ the man]] [$_{PP}$ with the binoculars]]

(20)
```
           VP
          /  \
        VP    PP
       /  \    △
      V    NP  with the binoculars
    watch  △
          the man
```

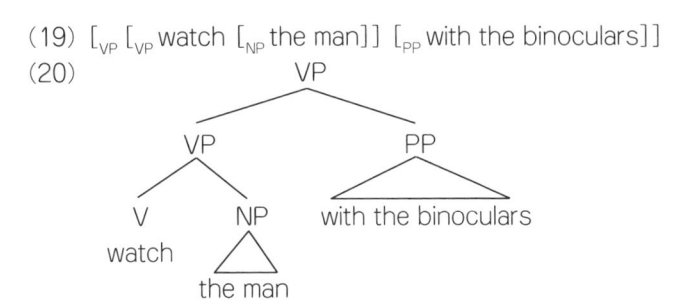

(20)では，with the binoculars は watch the man という VP を修飾している。

RETROSPECT AND PROSPECT

In this chapter, we have introduced the notion of constituent or syntactic unit, shown how constituents can be identified, distinguished between complements and adjuncts, seen that the phrases VP, NP, AP, and PP are all organized in essentially the same way, and shown how the constituent structure of a phrase can be represented in terms of a labeled bracketing or a tree diagram. We have so far said nothing about the structure of the sentence, however. Since we have emphasized that the verb and its object, if any, form a constituent that excludes the subject, one reasonable hypothesis would be that the basic structure of the sentence is as in (21), where we have used "S" to stand for "sentence" (compare (2) above).

hypothesis＝仮説

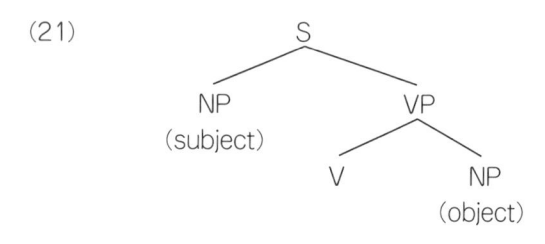

(21)
```
          S
         / \
        NP  VP
     (subject) / \
              V   NP
                (object)
```

In fact, (21) was for many years taken to represent the structure of the sentence, and is still for many purposes a reasonable approximation thereof. In the next chapter, however, in taking a closer look at sentence structure, we will find reason to postulate a structure for the sentence that is, while more complex than (21), also more regular in terms of the general picture of **phrase structure** we have sketched above.

phrase structure＝句構造

本文の理解を助けるために

統語論は現代言語学の中心となる重要な分野であるが，数学のようで取っつきにくいと思う人もいるだろう。そこで，本文の理解を助けるために，日本語で解説を付け加えておく。

枝分かれ構造と修飾関係

人間の言語の1つの特徴は，小さな要素が寄り集まって大きな階層構造を作っていくということである。第3章で挙げた American football fans という例を思い出してみよう。これは，区切り方によって，「アメリカンフットボールのファン」とも「アメリカ人のフットボールファン」とも理解できる。これは複合語を含む例であったが，句や文でも同じ考え方が成り立つ。more intelligent robots という例を考えてみよう。これは区切り方によって，2通りに解釈できる。

1. more intelligent / robots （もっと頭の良いロボット）
2. more / intelligent robots （もっと多くの，頭の良いロボット）

1の意味では more は intelligent だけに係って「もっと頭の良い」となるが，2の解釈では more は intelligent robots 全体に係る。階層構造を使うと，この修飾関係の違いを明確に表すことができる。

3.
more　　intelligent　　robots
もっと　　頭の良い　　　ロボット

4.
more　　intelligent　　robots
もっと多くの　頭の良い　　ロボット

3の図では，まず，more と intelligent が「もっと頭の良い」という意味のまとまり（「**構成素** constitutent」と言う）を形成し，それ全体が robots を修飾する。他方，4の図では，先に intelligent と robots がまとまって，「頭の良いロボット」という構成素を作り，それ全体に more が係っている。ここで注意が必要なのは，次のように3つの単語を一度に繋がないということである。

×
more　intelligent　robots

これでは，何が何を修飾するのかが明示されない。

3と4の図に示されるように，枝分かれ構造の成り立ちによって複数の意味解釈がなりたつことを**構造的曖昧性**（structural ambiguity）と言う。

構成素の見分け方

構成素は意味のまとまりを作っているが，統語論において重要なのは，構成素が全体として，「移動，削除，代用，等位接続」などの文法的な操作を受けるということである。本文では，このことを動詞句（VP）の例で説明している。ここでは，名詞句で説明してみよう。He likes this Japanese song. という文を例にとると，目的語の this Japanese song が1つの構成素であることは，「移動」と「代用」のテストを用いて証明できる。

(A) 移動のテスト：構成素は全体として移動される。It is X that… という強調構文（「分裂文」

と言う)で，X のところに入るのは 1 つの構成素に限られる。この性質を利用して，this Japanese song を X の位置に移動すると，正しく英文が成り立つ。

    It is this Japanese song that he likes.

他方，this Japanese song の一部分だけを移動すると，間違った英語になる。

    *It is song that he likes this Japanese.
    *It is Japanese song that he likes this.

同じように，目的語を文の先頭に移動させる「話題化」という構文がある。this Japanese song 全体を文頭に移動すると，次のように正しい英文ができる。

    This Japanese song, he likes.

しかし，一部分だけを移動すると非文になる。

    *This Japanese, he likes song.
    *Japanese song, he likes this.

(B) 代用のテスト：構成素は，全体を 1 つの代名詞で置き換えることができる。先ほどの例文で，目的語のthis Japanese song全体を代名詞(it)で置き換えることは問題なくできる。しかし，一部分の this Japanese や Japanese song だけを it で置き換えることはできない。

    He likes this Japanese song. → He likes it.
    *He likes this it. *He likes it song.

以上から，this Japanese song は 1 つの構成素になっていることが証明される。

樹形図の書き方

 上の 3, 4 に例示した枝分かれ構造は，ただ単に線(「枝(branch)」と言う)がつないであるだけだが，これでは，文における働き(つまり，動詞なのか名詞なのか形容詞なのかといった文法的な範疇)が分からない。そこで，まとまり(構成素)ごとに何らかの記号をつけて，文法的な働きを表すことが必要になる。

 枝分かれ構造で使われる記号には 2 種類ある。まず，1 つ 1 つの単語にはそれぞれの品詞(語彙範疇 lexical category)を表す記号が付く。品詞記号を一括して挙げておこう。

語彙範疇

 N(Noun＝名詞)：house, sugar, philosophy など

 V(Verb＝動詞)：build, eat, put, swim など

 A(Adjective＝形容詞)：intelligent, smart, happy, asleep など

 Av(Adverb＝副詞)：easily, slowly, happily, fast, hard など

 P(Preposition＝前置詞)：at, on, in, through, along, over など

 Q(Quantifier＝数量詞)：many, much, more, (a) few, little, three など

 D(Determiner＝限定詞)：冠詞の a, the, 指示詞の this, those, 所有格 my, his, her など

 先に挙げた more intelligent robots で試してみると，まず，第一ステップとして，5 と 6 のような構造ができるはずである。ここでは，2 つの解釈に応じて，more の働きが異なることに注意したい。つまり，数量詞(Q)である more が，intelligent の比較級を表す場合と，「もっと多くの」という数を表す場合の 2 通りである。

```
5.  Q           A              N          6.  Q           A              N
    |           |              |              |           |              |
   more     intelligent      robots         more      intelligent      robots
   もっと    頭の良い         ロボット       もっと多くの 頭の良い        ロボット
```

　第二ステップとしては，先ほど述べたように，意味のまとまりごとに線(枝)をつないで，枝と枝の交わったところ(「**節点** node」と言う)に何らかの記号をつける。枝と枝が交わるところは，もはや，一単語ではなく句(phrase)になっているから，記号も「○○Phrase」となる。これを**句範疇**(phrasal category)と言う。句範疇の作り方は，細かく言うと複雑になるので，ここでは最も単純な方法を述べておく。

句範疇

NP(Noun Phrase＝名詞句)：
　名詞(N)を軸として，その前(あるいは後ろ)に修飾語句が付いたまとまり。
　my book, this interesting book, little sugar, coffee with cream など。

VP(Verb Phrase＝動詞句)：
　動詞(V)を軸として，その後ろ(あるいは前)に目的語，補語，副詞などが付いたまとまり。
　read this book, look at the star, run fast など。

AP(Adjective Phrase：形容詞句)：
　形容詞を軸として，その前(あるいは後ろ)に修飾語句が付いたまとまり。
　very good, fond of music など。

AvP(Adverb Phrase：副詞句)：
　副詞を軸としたまとまり。very fortunately など。

PP(Prepositional Phrase：前置詞句)：
　前置詞の後に名詞が付いたまとまり。in the room, with a knife など。

これを more intelligent robots の例に当てはめると，まず，小さなまとまりを見つけて枝をつなぐ。

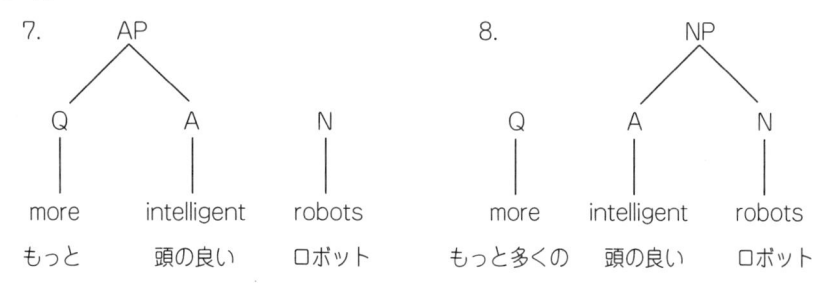

```
7.        AP                      8.            NP
         /  \                                  /  \
        Q    A      N                   Q     A    N
        |    |      |                   |     |    |
      more intelligent robots         more intelligent robots
      もっと 頭の良い  ロボット        もっと多くの 頭の良い ロボット
```

7 では more intelligent が AP(形容詞句)を形成し，他方，8 では intelligent robots が NP(名詞句)を形成する。
　引き続いて，残った単語をつないで，もう1つ上のまとまりを作ると，次のようになる。

```
9.          NP                      10.         NP
       ┌────┼────┐                        ┌──────┴──┐
      AP         N                                  NP
     ┌─┴─┐       │                        ┌─────────┼────┐
     Q   A       N                        Q         A    N
     │   │       │                        │         │    │
   more intelligent robots              more    intelligent robots
   もっと 頭の良い  ロボット              もっと多くの 頭の良い  ロボット
```

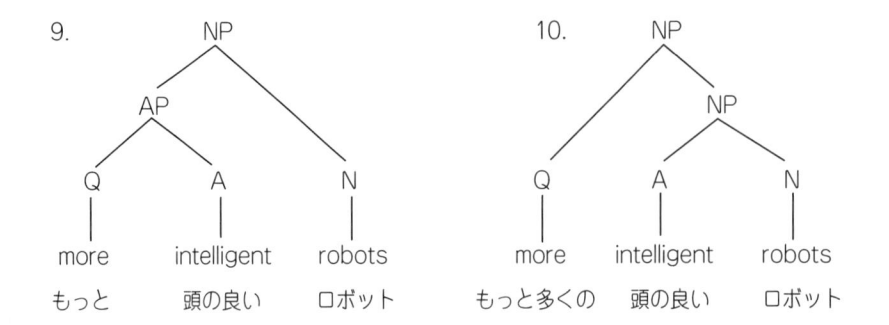

9の図では，NPが二階建てになっている。最新の理論では，これとは違う記号が使われるのだが，この入門書では，NPやVPが二階建て，三階建てになっても良いことにしておく。すると，9も10も，全体としては名詞句(NP)になる。すなわち，どちらの構造も，主要部であるrobotsという名詞のことを述べているわけである。

　最後に，冠詞に触れておこう。冠詞には定冠詞(the)と不定冠詞(a, an)があるが，どちらも名詞句の先頭に現れる。その点では，指示詞(this, these)と所有格(my, his)も同じである。しかも，1つの名詞については，これらはいずれか1つしか使われない。「私の，この帽子」を直訳して，*my this hatとすると間違った英語になる。aとhis, theとthatなども一緒には使えない。つまり，英語では，冠詞，指示詞，所有格は同じ働きの単語であり，使うときはどれか1つを選ばなければならないわけである。そこで，冠詞，指示詞，所有格をまとめて**限定詞**(Determiner)と呼ぶ。限定詞は，名詞句の一番先頭，つまり，枝分かれ構造では一番上の位置に現れる。

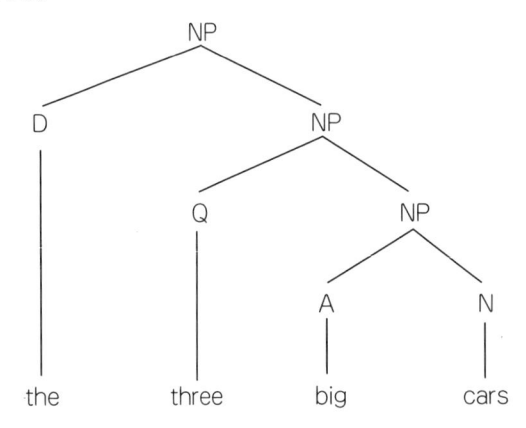

```
              NP
         ┌────┴────┐
         D         NP
         │     ┌───┴───┐
         │     Q       NP
         │     │    ┌──┴──┐
         │     │    A     N
         │     │    │     │
        the  three big   cars
```

　以上のように，枝分かれ構造を書くときには，意味の小さなまとまりを先に見つけて，そのまとまりに小さな山形をつける。大きなまとまりは，それより上に山形を作る。下から上に，この作業を続けていけば，どのような複雑な文でも枝分かれ構造で表すことができる。

五文型と枝分かれ構造

　たいていの人は，高校の英文法で，SV, SVC, SVO, SVOO, SVOCという五文型を習ったことだろう。これは便利な面もあるが，言語学的に厳密に言うと不適切な面のほうが多い。もっとも大きな欠点は，主語(S)，動詞(V)，目的語(O)，補語(C)を単に横一列に並べているだけであるという点である。文の要(かなめ)となるのは動詞である。動詞が他動詞なら目的語が現れ，自動詞なら目的語はつかない。従って，文型を考える際には動詞を軸(専門用語では**主**

要部(head))として捉える必要がある。五文型のもう 1 つの欠点は，どの文型にも主語(S)が出ているということである。英語では，主語のない文は(命令文以外)成り立たないから，わざわざ S をつける必要はない。主語を除くと，五文型は次のように整理できる。

1. V （cry や rise のように，主語をつけるだけで済む動詞）
2. V C （look sad や look at him のように補語ないし前置詞句を伴う動詞）
3. V O （build a house のように目的語を一つ取る動詞）
4. V O O （send him a letter のように二重目的語を取る動詞）
5. V O C （consider him honest のように目的語と補語を取る動詞）

分かりやすい例として，VO 文型と VC 文型で説明しよう。

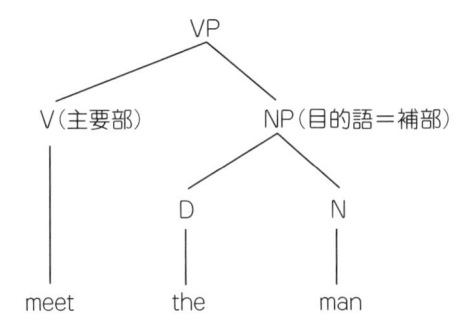

```
                VP
              /    \
         V(主要部)   NP(目的語＝補部)
            |       /    \
                   D      N
                   |      |
          meet    the    man
```

meet the man という VO 文型では，主要部は動詞 meet である。主要部が文法的に必要とする要素を**補部**(complement)と呼ぶと，meet という他動詞にとっては the man という目的語が補部である。同じ考え方を depend on the man のような自動詞に適用すると，depend という動詞にとって必要なのは on〜 という前置詞句であるから，これが補部となる。

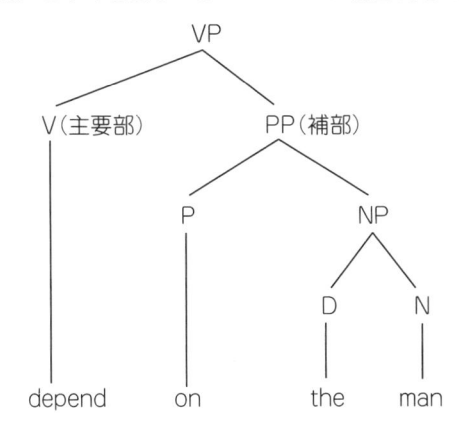

```
                 VP
              /      \
         V(主要部)   PP(補部)
            |        /    \
                    P      NP
                    |     /  \
                         D    N
                         |    |
         depend   on    the   man
```

最後に，VP の上に主語を継ぎ足すと，文(Sentence)になる。

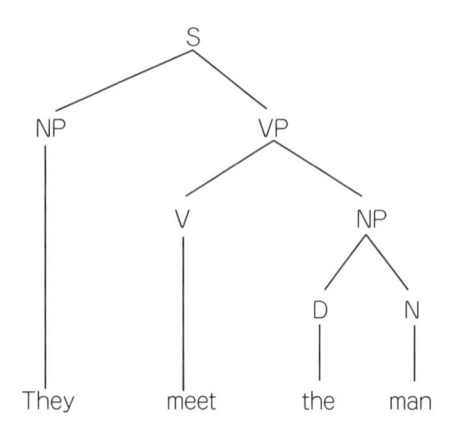

```
          S
         / \
        NP  VP
        |   / \
        |  V   NP
        |  |   / \
        |  |  D   N
        |  |  |   |
       They meet the man
```

なお，第 6 章では助動詞も含めて文の構造を更に詳しく説明している。

補部と付加部

　補部が動詞にとって必要な要素であるとすると，あってもなくてもよい副詞的な要素は**付加部**(adjunct)と呼ばれ，補部とは異なる構造位置にあると考えられている。

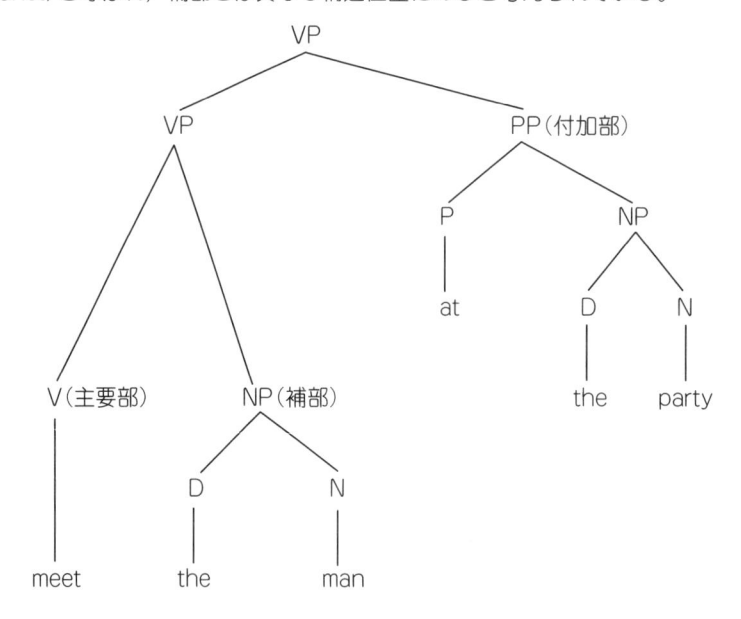

```
              VP
             /  \
            VP   PP(付加部)
           /  \    / \
          /    \  P   NP
         /      \ |   / \
        V(主要部) NP(補部) at D   N
         |      / \      |   |
        meet   D   N    the party
               |   |
              the man
```

　補部は主要部にとって意味的に必要な要素であるから，この意味の性質が枝分かれ構造にも反映されて，補部(the man)は主要部(meet)とおなじ階層にある(同じ階層にあるものを姉妹(sister)と言う)。これに対して，「パーティーで」という副詞的な要素(付加部)は動詞とは結びつきが弱いので，構造上も，動詞がある階層(下の方の VP)とは別の，上の VP に付けられる。要するに，V(主要部)と補部がまとまって VP という構成素を作り，付加部はその上に VP を重ねて(何段にも)積み上げられる。

Comprehension Check

✎ 空所を埋めなさい。

　文の組み立て方を研究する分野は（　　　）と呼ばれる。英語の文は，主語，動詞，目的語が横一列に並んでいるのではなく，上下関係のある（　　　）構造を構成している。とりわけ，動詞は目的語と一緒になって（　　　）というまとまりを構成し，主語はそれより上の階層に現れる。このような構造を仮定すると，意味上の修飾関係が端的に表される。例えば，p.46(3)は，形容詞の smart がどの名詞に係るかによって2つの構造が区別できる。p.46(5a)の構造は（　　　）と（　　　）の両方が smart な場合であり，(5b)の構造は（　　　）だけが smart な場合である。このような統語的なまとまりを（　　　）と呼ぶ。ひと繋がりの単語がまとまりを形成するかどうかは，意味上の修飾関係だけでなく，統語的には（　　　），（　　　），（　　　），（　　　）などのテストで確かめることができる。

　句(phrase)の中で中心となる要素を（　　　）と言い，それと緊密に関係する要素を（　　　）と呼ぶ。他動詞の場合，例えば build に対する a house のような目的語（名詞句）がそれに当たり，自動詞の場合は，look と組み合わされる at the flower や depend と組み合わされる on the teacher のような（　　　）句がそれに当たる。これらは，それぞれの動詞にとって文法的に必要な要素であり，結びつきが個々の動詞によって決まっている。build は他動詞であるから必ず a house のような目的語が必要であり，look や depend のような自動詞の場合も，それぞれどのような（　　　）句と結びつくかが決まっている。これに対して，on Sunday のような副詞的な表現は，単なる修飾句であり，（　　　）と呼ばれる。これは，特定の動詞だけに限られるわけではなく，どのような動詞とでも一緒に用いられるから，動詞にとっては，あまり重要な要素ではない。このような重要性の違いは，樹形図の上下関係で表される。すなわち，（　　　）と（　　　）は，構造上，「姉妹関係」（枝分かれ図において同じ階層にある関係）を構成し，（　　　）はそれより上の階層につく。

Exercises

(1) 移動と代用のテストを用いて，次の例文の下線部が構成素(constituent)になっているかどうかを判定しなさい。

　　a. I watched <u>the man</u> with the binoculars.（「双眼鏡で見た」という意味）
　　b. I watched <u>the man with the binoculars</u>.（「双眼鏡を持った男」という意味）
　　c. My uncle gave <u>all the Japanese dolls</u> to the American girl.
　　d. My uncle gave <u>the American girl all the Japanese dolls</u>.

    e.　Her husband has gone to Africa.
    f.　We are supposed to meet in the hotel at three o'clock.
    g.　We are supposed to meet in the hotel at three o'clock in the afternoon.

(2) The girls play the game in the room on Sundays. という例文の統語構造を樹形図で示しなさい。［ヒント：on Sundays という時間の付加部は，in the room という場所の付加部より更に上のVPに付くものとする。］

(3) A. 本文(14a)で，She refused. という文の refused は，一語であるが，単に動詞(V)であるだけでなく，動詞句(VP)でもあると説明した。そうすると，この refused の部分はどのような構造になるのだろうか。樹形図で表しなさい。

　　B. 同じように，She likes this song. の this song が名詞句(NP)とすると，She likes music. の music は，一語の名詞(N)であるが，同時に名詞句(NP)でもある。（一般に，主語や目的語になるのは名詞句である。）このことを踏まえて，She likes music. の動詞句(likes music)がどのような構造になるか示しなさい。

(4) 次の例の統語構造を樹形図で表しなさい。

    a.　a very tall tree
    b.　very fond of Japanese food ［ヒント：of ～ は fond の補部とする。］
    c.　The train arrived at the station on time.
    d.　My sister bought this skirt at that store.
    e.　The boy cried in the bathroom at night.
    f.　I saw the man with binoculars with my own binoculars.

(5) 次の例文は，on the table の取り方によって2通りに解釈できる。

　　The boy jumped on the table.
　　A. 2通りの意味を日本語で説明し，その構造的あいまい性を樹形図で表示しなさい。［ヒント：onがontoの意味のときは，補部として扱うことにする。］
　　B. 上の例文で on the table を文頭に持っていって，On the table, the boy jumped. とすると，曖昧性はなくなる。その場合，どのような意味になるだろうか。

(6) 次の A と B は動詞が違うだけで，一見，同じように見える。まず日本語に訳してみよう。

    A. The girl put on the boots. （　　　　　　　　　）
    B. The girl sat on the boots. （　　　　　　　　　）

A と B の構造を簡略化して，アとイに示す（P は preposition（前置詞）または particle（小辞。高校の英文法では「副詞」として習ったもの）を表す）。"on" の働きに注目して，どちらがどちらの構造に当てはまるか答えなさい。（イの図で，V の下に V と P があるのは，V と P が「句動詞 phrasal verb」として，いわば複合動詞のようなまとまりになっているということを表している。）

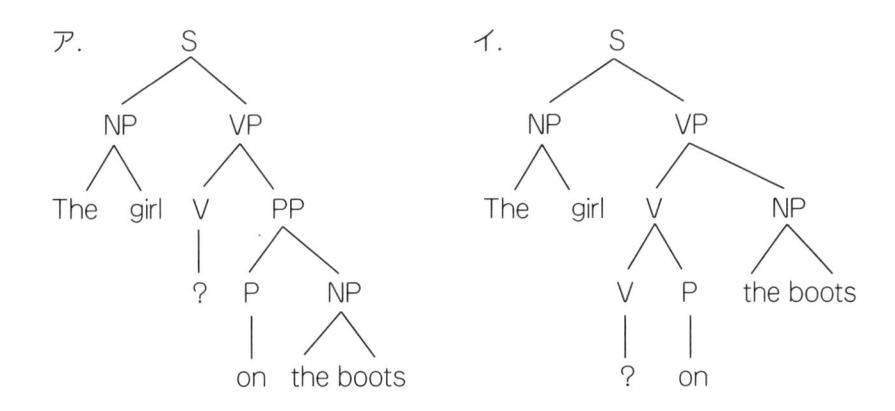

ア．
```
           S
          / \
        NP   VP
       /\    /\
   The girl V  PP
            |  /\
            ? P  NP
              |  /\
              on the boots
```

イ．
```
           S
          / \
        NP   VP
       /\    /\
   The girl V  NP
            /\  |
           V  P the boots
           |  |
           ?  on
```

構成素の性質を用いて，自分が割り当てた構造が本当に正しいかどうか，検証してみよう。次の各組で，英語として正しい文に○，間違っている文に✕を付け，それに基づいて，自分が選んだ構造が正しいことを論証しなさい。

1. 強調構文における「移動」
    a. (　　) It was <u>on the boots</u> that the girl put.
    b. (　　) It was <u>on the boots</u> that the girl sat.
2. 一語の there による「代用」
    a. (　　) The girl put <u>there</u>.
    b. (　　) The girl sat <u>there</u>.
3. 等位接続
    a. (　　) The girl put both <u>on the stockings</u> and <u>on the boots</u>.
    b. (　　) The girl sat both <u>on the hat</u> and <u>on the boots</u>.

(7) 次の例文は構造的に曖昧である。それぞれについて，2 通りの意味解釈を説明し，意味の違いが統語構造に反映されるように樹形図で書き表しなさい。

    a.   The teacher read her books.
    b.   The girl read the letter to her friend.

(8) 次の樹形図に自由に英語の単語を当てはめ，意味の通る英文を作りなさい。

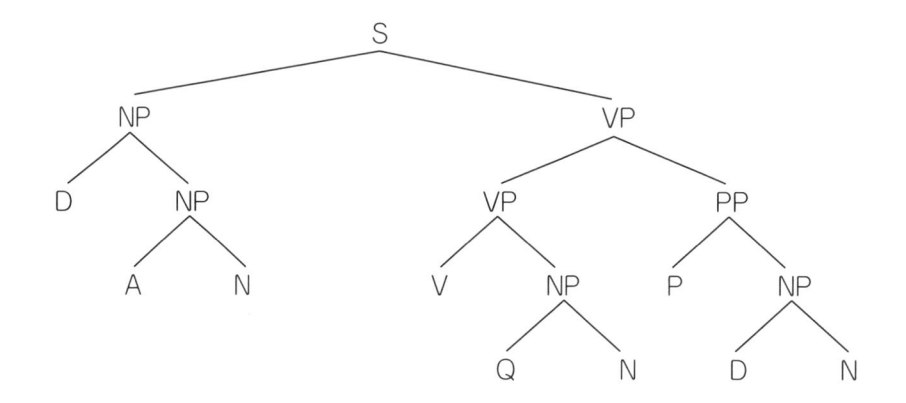

```
                      S
             ┌────────┴────────┐
            NP                 VP
          ┌──┴──┐         ┌────┴────┐
          D    NP         VP        PP
              ┌─┴─┐     ┌──┴──┐   ┌──┴──┐
              A   N     V    NP   P    NP
                            ┌┴┐       ┌┴┐
                            Q N       D N
```

Chapter 6 How English Sentences Are Formed: Syntax II

> **BASIC QUESTIONS**
> Jim has left, Sue will sing の助動詞 has や will は, 枝分かれ構造でどのような位置にあるのだろうか。また, I know that Jim has left, I wonder if Sue is singing の that や if はどのような単語だろうか。Has Jim left?, When is Sue singing? のような疑問文における助動詞の位置はどのように説明できるのだろうか。

AUXILIARY VERBS, TENSE, AND THE TENSE ELEMENT T

In this chapter, we will examine the structure of the English sentence or **clause**, considering several hypotheses before settling on one that seems to fit all the facts. Our starting point will be (1), an abbreviated version of the tentative proposal concerning sentence structure that we made at the end of Chapter 5 (in the present chapter, we will ignore the internal structure of VP).

clause =
節 (ここでは文 (sentence) と同じこと)
hypotheses =
仮説 (hypothesis の複数形)
tentative = 暫定的な

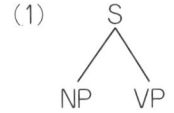

(1)   S
     /\
   NP VP

We may note immediately that examples like (2a) and (2b) are not covered by (1), since they contain an **auxiliary verb** between the NP *the girl* and the VP *refuse/refused the offer*.

auxiliary verb = 助動詞

(2) a. The girl **will** refuse the offer.
    b. The girl **has** refused the offer.

The suggestion that the auxiliaries *will* and *has* of (2) are not part of VP receives support from the fact that those auxiliaries are not affected by **VP-deletion**. Thus, consider (3a) and (3b), where the bracketed VP is subject to deletion:

VP-deletion = 動詞句削除

(3) a. Sue will refuse the offer, and Jim will [refuse the offer] too.
    b. Sue has refused the offer, and Jim has [refused the offer] too.

As you can see, the auxiliaries *will* and *has* remain even when the VP *refuse/refused the offer* is deleted.

We have seen that there is a syntactic element between NP and VP in examples with auxiliary verbs like those of (2). In fact, it

syntactic element =
統語的要素

is possible to show that there is a syntactic element between NP and VP even in sentences without auxiliary verbs. Thus, consider examples (4a) and (4b), where (4b) is the result of applying VP-deletion to the second clause of (4a) (as in the examples of (3), we have bracketed the material that apparently undergoes deletion).

(4) a. Jim likes the Beatles, and his father [liked the Beatles] too.
b. Jim likes the Beatles, and his father **did** too.

Note that (4b) contains an auxiliary verb *do* that is not present in (4a). We will assume that this is the same *do* that appears in **questions** like *Do you like the Beatles?* and **negative** sentences like *I do not like the Beatles*, and that it is the result of a rule inserting *do* (***do*-insertion**) in a special set of environments. While it will not be possible in this chapter to consider the entire set of environments in which *do* is inserted, we will be able to get a fairly good idea of why insertion takes place in cases like (4b).

Let us ask what (4b) looks like before undergoing VP-deletion. One possibility, of course, is that it looks like (4a). There are two problems, however, with postulating (4a) as the pre-VP-deletion form of (4b). One is that, although deletion of a VP can normally take place only when there is an identical VP elsewhere in the linguistic context, the bracketed material in (4a) is not identical to anything else in that sentence. The second and more serious problem is that if the bracketed material of (4a) is removed, there will be no way to tell that the **tense** of the inserted auxiliary *do* is to be past rather than present. Both of these problems can be avoided if we postulate a more abstract structure like (5), where the tense (PRES(ENT) or PAST) is represented separately from VP.

(5) Jim PRES [$_{VP}$ like the Beatles], and his father PAST [$_{VP}$ like the Beatles] too.

In (5), PRES and PAST, which stand for present tense and past tense, respectively, are abstract elements that must combine with some verb, main or auxiliary, in order to be pronounced or "phonetically realized."

Consider what will happen when the second occurrence of the VP *like the Beatles* is deleted in (5). The elements PRES and PAST will be unaffected, and the result will be (6).

phonetically realized = 音声的に具現される

(6) Jim PRES [$_{VP}$ like the Beatles], and his father PAST ~~like the Beatles~~ too.

In the first clause of (6), the element PRES will combine with the verb *like*, and, since the subject is third person singular, the result will be *likes*. The element PAST in the second clause, however, will have no verb to combine with. It is for this reason that *do* is inserted. Since insertion of *do* takes place to "support" the tense element, the insertion process is sometimes called "*do*-support." The final result will be (4b), repeated below as (7).

(7) Jim likes the Beatles, and his father did too.
　　(PRES+like=likes, PAST+*do*=did)

With the symbol T standing for a syntactic element that contains a specification for tense (either PRES or PAST), we may thus hypothesize that the basic clause structure of English is NP + T + VP, where the first auxiliary verb, if any, occurs in T along with the tense specification. At this point, a representation of the basic structure we are postulating for an English sentence will therefore look like (8).

specification = 指定
hypothesize = 仮定する

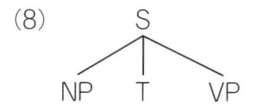

(8)
```
        S
      / | \
    NP  T  VP
```

COMPLEX SENTENCES, THE ELEMENT C, AND MOVEMENT

While the hypothesis of (8) might seem adequate for simple sentences, it will not cover examples like those of (9):

(9) a.　Jim knows **that** Sue has won the election.
　　b.　Jim wonders **if** Sue has won the election.
　　c.　Jim would prefer **for** Sue to win the election.

The sentences of (9) each contain two NP + T + VP combinations linked by an element *that, if,* or *for.* It is those linking elements, called **complementizers** because they introduce a clause that functions as the complement of the preceding verb, that are not covered by the formulation NP + T + VP. Using **C** to stand for "complementizer," we thus propose, as our next hypothesis, that in the general case, an English clause (either "independent" or "dependent") contains the elements C + NP + T + VP.

complementizer = 補文標識(補文を導くための that, if は学校文法では接続詞と呼ばれる。不定詞の意味上の主語を表す for も補文標識)

independent clause = 独立節
dependent clause = 従属節

Interestingly, complementizers are not the only items that can occur in the C position of a clause. Consider (10a) and (10b), which are synonymous:

(10) a. If I had known that, I would have stayed at home.
　　 b. Had I known that, I would have stayed at home.

conditional clause = 条件節

(10a) begins with a **conditional clause** introduced by *if.* We will assume that this *if*, like that of (9a), is in C. What (10b) shows is that under certain circumstances, the first auxiliary verb of a conditional clause can appear before rather than after the subject, and that when it does so, it replaces *if*. We will interpret this as showing that the first auxiliary (*had*) can move from T, its normal position, across the subject to C, as shown in (11).

(11)　　C　　NP　　T　　　VP
　　　 [ ]　　I　　had　　known that

The reason we assume that the auxiliary moves to C is that if it moved to some other position, it should be able to occur together with *if*. (12a) and (12b), however, show that this is impossible:

(12) a. *If had I known that, ...
　　 b. *Had if I known that, ...

construction = 構文

T-to-C movement = T から C への移動

The first auxiliary of a sentence appears before the subject, however, not only in conditional clauses like that of (10b), but also in questions and several other constructions. If we extend to all such cases the **T-to-C movement** account just proposed for (10b), it follows that the auxiliaries *will* and *did* of (13) will be in C as well:

(13) a. **Will** Sue refuse the offer?
     b. **Did** Sue refuse the offer?

The same will be true of the auxiliaries *has* and *should* of (14):

(14) a. Which offer **has** Sue refused?
     b. On what grounds **should** Sue refuse the offer?

In the examples of (14), however, there is an additional phrase before the auxiliary in C, an NP (*which offer*) in (14a) and a PP (*on what grounds*) in (14b). This phrase, like the auxiliary, can be shown to have moved from a position to the right of the subject (***wh*-movement**). In the case of (14a), for example, this is because *which offer* is understood as the object of the verb *refused*. The movement that we are assuming in (14a), then, is as shown in (15).

wh-movement =
wh 移動 (疑問詞を含む句の移動)

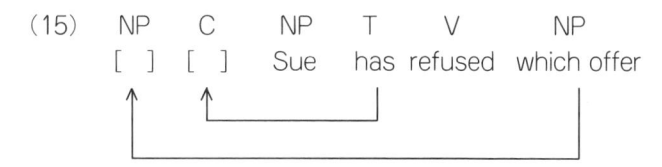

(15) NP   C   NP   T   V   NP
      [ ] [ ] Sue   has refused which offer

Abbreviating the **interrogative phrase** that occurs before C as "XP," we arrive at (16) as our final proposal for the sequence of elements that enter into the basic clause structure of English. (16) includes the two abstract **functional heads** T and C.

interrogative phrase =
疑問詞

functional head =
機能的主要部 (lexical head
語彙的主要部と対照)

(16)   XP+C+NP+T+VP

THE INTERNAL STRUCTURE OF THE SEQUENCE OF SUB-CLAUSAL ELEMENTS

The way we have written the sequence (16) suggests that these five elements are simply strung together in a row. Given what we learned about constituent structure in Chapter 5, however, this would seem unlikely. In fact, it can be shown that the sequence (16) has a complex internal structure.

The sequence T + VP, first of all, would seem to be a constituent, as indicated by the coordination test we saw in Chapter 5:

(17) That student both [has failed to meet minimum academic standards] and [is creating a disturbance in class].

There is no doubt that the sequence NP + T + VP, which corresponds to the simple sentence, is also a constituent. Finally, the coordination test indicates that the sequence C + NP + T + VP is a constituent as well:

(18) Jim thinks both [that Sue will win the election]
                   and [that she will make a superb governor].

(16) thus has the bracketed structure [XP [C [NP [T VP]]]]. The remaining question is that of the **category** or label of the various subconstituents.

(NP +) T + VP sequences can be classified according to whether they are **finite** or **infinitival**, and (XP +) C + NP + T + VP sequences can be classified according to whether they are **declarative** or **interrogative** (i.e. statements or questions) as well. This is illustrated in (19), where these three types of sequences are enclosed in brackets:

(19) a. Jim thinks [that [Sue [will win the election]]].
    b. Jim would like [for [Sue [to win the election]]].
    c. Jim wonders [if [Sue [will win the election]]].

The C + NP + T + VP combination of (19a) is finite and declarative, that of (19b) is infinitival and declarative, and that of (19c) is finite and interrogative. Further, it is clearly the T and C elements of these sequences — *that* and *will* in (19a), *for* and *to* in (19b), and *if* and *will* in (19c) — that determine these characteristics. As a result, it is natural to take T to be the head of T + VP (and of NP + T + VP), and to take C to be the head of C + NP + T + VP (and of XP + C + NP + T + VP). If we call the largest constituent with head Y (for any Y) "YP" (Y-phrase), this will mean that the NP + T + VP combination, what we called "S" in (1) and (8) above, will become **TP**, and that the XP + C + NP + T + VP combination will become **CP**. We also need a label for a constituent with head Y intermediate in size between Y and YP, since T + VP and C + TP are both constituents of this type. Using, as is customary, **Y´** (read "Y-bar") for such a constituent, the structure of an English clause becomes [$_{CP}$ XP [$_{C'}$ C [$_{TP}$ NP [$_{T'}$ T VP]]]] or, in tree-diagram form, (20):

(20)
```
         CP
        /  \
      XP    C'
           /  \
          C    TP
              /  \
             NP   T'
                 /  \
                T    VP
```

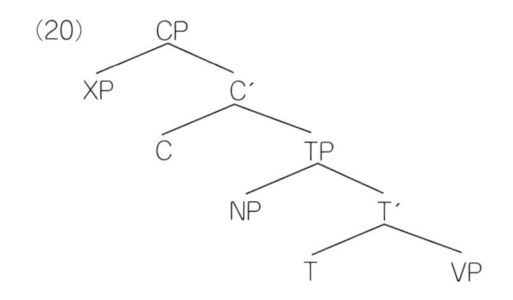

XP は疑問詞が入る位置

NP は主語が入る位置

Let us compare (20) with the structure in (1) that served as our starting point. (20) is a good deal more complex than (1), but one reason for this is that it covers the elements XP (the moved interrogative phrase of questions) and C. The portion of (20) that should in fact be compared with (1) (reproduced below) is the portion from TP downward, which is displayed in (21).

(21)
```
      TP
     /  \
    NP   T'
        /  \
       T    VP
```

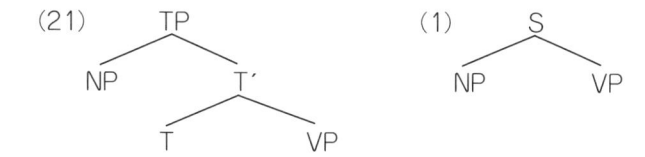

(1)
```
      S
     / \
    NP  VP
```

(21), like (20), is more complex than (1), but it is also more regular. Remember that we saw in Chapter 5 that phrase structure is generally **headed** — that is, that phrases have heads. Thus, the head of VP is V, the head of NP is N, the head of AP is A, and the head of PP is P. But S in (1) is a glaring exception to this rule. Under the analysis of (1), in other words, the sentence is not headed. The analysis of (21) eliminates this irregularity, because it analyzes S as TP — that is, as a constituent whose head is T. In this sense, the analysis of (21) (and, more generally, of (20)) represents an important step toward a simple and general theory of phrase structure.

headed = 主要部を持っている

CLAUSE STRUCTURE AND HISTORICAL WORD-ORDER CHANGE

In conclusion, let us observe that the structure (20) provides a natural way of understanding the historical word-order variation that we observed at the end of Chapter 2. There, we noted examples like (22) and (23), where the verb (double underline) precedes, in Shakespeare's English and earlier, various items (single underline) which, in contemporary English, it follows (modern equivalents are given in parentheses):

(22) a. The erthe and the lond <u><u>chaungeth</u></u> <u>often</u> his colour. (<u>often</u> <u><u>change</u></u>)
   b. I <u><u>think</u></u> <u>not</u> of them. (do <u>not</u> <u><u>think</u></u>)
   c. Let them <u><u>fly</u></u> <u>all</u>. (let them <u>all</u> <u><u>fly</u></u>)
(23) a. <u><u>Ride</u></u> <u>you</u> this afternoon? (Do <u>you</u> <u><u>ride</u></u>)
   b. What <u><u>care</u></u> <u>I</u>, if ⋯ (What do <u>I</u> <u><u>care</u></u>)

The position of the doubly underlined main verbs in (22) and (23), however, is precisely that of auxiliary verbs in the modern language. This is shown by the examples of (24)-(25), which correspond one-to-one with those of (22)-(23):

(24) a. He <u><u>has</u></u> <u>often</u> changed his stand.
   b. I <u><u>have</u></u> <u>not</u> thought of them.
   c. They <u><u>have</u></u> <u>all</u> fled.
(25) a. <u><u>Have</u></u> <u>you</u> ridden this afternoon?
   b. <u><u>Have</u></u> <u>I</u> ever cared about that?

In this chapter, we have seen that the auxiliaries of (24) occur to the left of VP in the tense element T and that it is because (the item in) T moves to C in questions that the auxiliaries of (25) appear to the left of the subject. What the examples of (22) and (23) show, then, is that up to the time of Shakespeare, the same was true of main verbs as well. Until roughly the seventeenth century, in other words, main verbs moved to the left out of VP into T, and from there moved on to C in questions and certain other constructions. The fact that in Modern English this is true only of auxiliary verbs is one of the major differences between the early modern and the contemporary stages of the language.

本文の理解を助けるために

助動詞とdo挿入

動詞句削除(VP deletion)は，次のように，前と重複する動詞句を消す操作である。

1. John will [_VP_ go to school tomorrow], but Peter won't [_VP_ ~~go to school tomorrow~~].
2. If John can [_VP_ solve this problem], Peter can [_VP_ ~~solve this problem~~] too.

1の例では，will/won't が助動詞であり，その後の go to school tomorrow が重複するから，この部分(VP)が削除される。2 でも同じように，solve this problem という部分が動詞句であり，これが削除される。2 の例で注意したいのは，助動詞 can も重複しているのに，can は削除できないという点である。2 の文で，Peter の後の can まで一緒に消すと，英語として間違った文(3)になってしまう。

3. *If John can solve this problem, Peter too.

このことから，動詞句削除をするときは，主語のあとに助動詞があることが必要であることが分かる。普通，助動詞というと will や can などの**法助動詞**(modal auxiliary verb)を指すが，is, are などの **be** 動詞(John is smart, and Peter is too; Jim is dancing, but Tom isn't)と**完了形**の have(John hasn't solved the problem, but Peter has.)も同じ働きをする。いま仮に，これらの助動詞が入る位置をT(Tense：時制)で表すと，Peter can solve this problem. の構造は次のようになる。

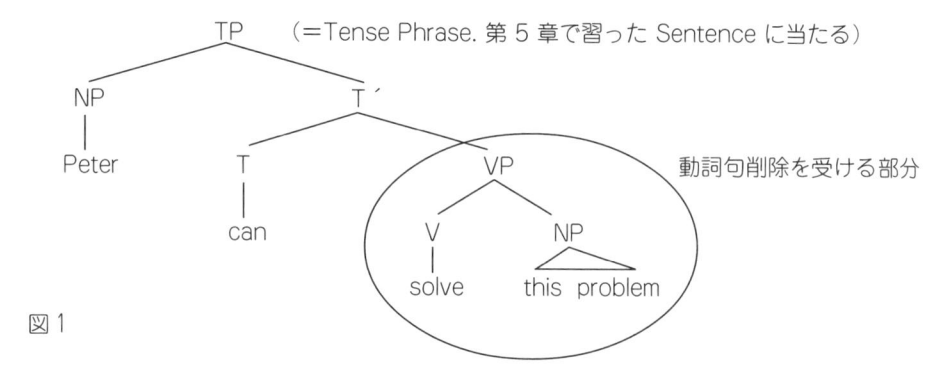

```
              TP      (=Tense Phrase. 第5章で習った Sentence に当たる)
           ／＼
          NP    T´
          │   ／＼
         Peter T    VP          動詞句削除を受ける部分
              │   ／＼
             can  V    NP
                  │    △
                solve this problem
```

図1

図1の構造に動詞句削除を適用すると，Peter can. となり，適格な英文ができる。

では，もし T の位置に何も助動詞がなければ，どうなるだろうか？

4. *John doesn't [_VP_ like classical music], but Peter [_VP_ ~~likes classical music~~].
5. *John didn't take the course, though all his friends [_VP_ ~~took the course~~].

4と5で単純に後ろ側の VP を削除すると，主語(Peter, all his friends)が残るだけで，助動詞がないから，非文となる。4, 5 を正しい英語にするためには，次のように，does, did を補う必要がある(**do挿入**と言う)。

6. John doesn't [_VP_ like classical music], but Peter does [_VP_ ~~like classical music~~].
7. John didn't [_VP_ take the course], though all his friends did [_VP_ ~~take the course~~].

6と7は，Peter does/all his friends did という正しい英語になるだけでなく，それぞれ，前の VP と後ろの VP が全く同じ形になるという点でも都合がよい。

さて，T というのは，現在 PRES(ENT)あるいは過去 PAST という時制を表す働きで，普通なら，時制は動詞に付く屈折語尾として表示される。

8. Peter PAST＋solve the problem. → Peter solved the problem.
9. John PRES＋like jazz. → John likes jazz.

ところが，動詞句が削除されると，屈折語尾を担うべき動詞がなくなってしまい，時制を表すことができない。PAST あるいは PRES という抽象的な要素はそのままでは発音できないから，それを助けるために do が挿入される。

●do 挿入：Tense を表す単語がないときだけ，do が挿入される。

Peter [$_T$ PAST] [$_{VP}$ solve the problem]

動詞句削除 → Peter [$_T$ PAST] [$_{VP}$ ~~solve the problem~~]

do 挿入 → Peter [$_T$ PAST+do] = Peter [$_T$ did]

do 挿入は，**do support** とも呼ばれるが，do が時制を支える(supportする)わけである。そのため，普通の平叙文に do 挿入を当てはめると，特別に時制を強調することになる。

10. Peter díd solve the problem.（did にアクセントを置く）

このように，法助動詞と，do 挿入の do とは構造上，同じ位置を占めるとすると，両者を同時に使うことができないことも納得がいく。

11. a. *Peter can do solve the problem.
    b. *Peter does can solve the problem.

疑問文における倒置

He can solve the problem. から Can he solve the problem? という疑問文を作るとき，主語と助動詞の位置が入れ替わる。学校文法ではこれを「倒置」と呼んでいるが，実は，主語は動かずに，Tの要素(can)が主語の前へ移動しているだけである。

●疑問文における T の移動

[　] Peter [$_T$ can] solve the problem?

can などの法助動詞だけでなく，be 動詞と完了形 have も同じように，主語の前へ移動する。もし T の位置に法助動詞も be も have もなくて，単に PRES または PAST という要素があるだけのときは，その要素が移動する。

[　] Peter [$_T$ PAST] solve the problem?

すると，PAST だけでは発音できないから，do 挿入が起こり，Did Peter solve the problem? となる。

補文（従属節）の構造

では，疑問文で助動詞が移動していく先（主語の前）というのは，どのような位置なのだろうか？　それを説明するために，まず，従属節の構造を見てみよう。

12. I believe that Peter can solve the problem.
13. I don't know if Peter can solve the problem.

主節の動詞(believe, know)と補文（従属節）をつなぐ that や if は，学校文法では接続詞と呼ばれるが，生成文法では**補文標識**（Complementizer; C）と言い，図 2 のような構造を取る。

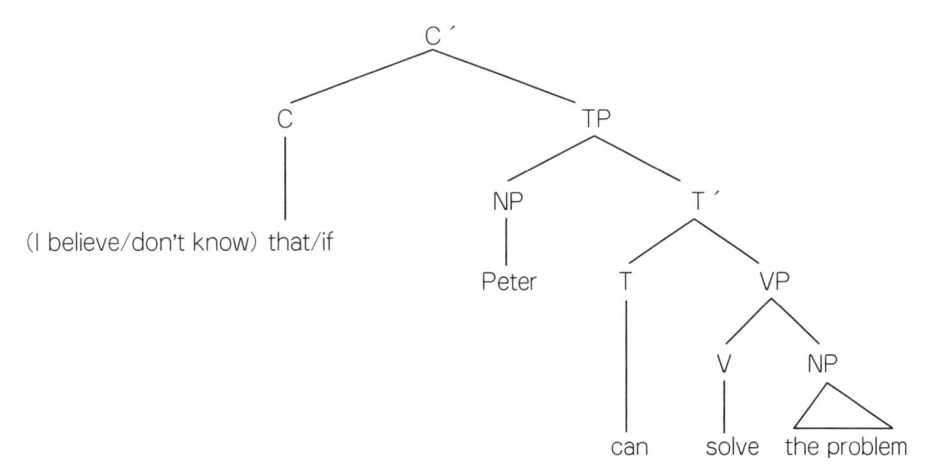

```
                        C´
                       / \
                      C   TP
                      |   / \
         (I believe/don't know) that/if
                         NP    T´
                         |    / \
                        Peter T   VP
                              |   / \
                              |  V   NP
                              |  |   /\
                              can solve the problem
```

図2

ところで，that, if などの補文標識は従属節では現れるが，主節(14)では現れない。

 14. *If he can solve the problem?
 15. Can he solve the problem?

正しくは，15 のように if が現れる位置（主語の前）に，助動詞 can が移動しなければならない。if が現れるか，can が主語の前に移動するかは，どちらか一方であって，両方同時には成り立たない。

 16. *I don't know if can he solve the problem.

つまり，if がない場合（主節の場合）にだけ，助動詞（T）の移動が起こる。言い換えると，15 の疑問文で，can が移動する先は，if/that が占めるのと同じ位置（すなわち C）であるということになる。

●T から C への移動

 [$_C$] he   [$_T$ can] [$_{VP}$ solve the problem]

本文 p. 66 では，この「T から C への移動」が疑問文だけでなく，if のない仮定節 (If I had known that → Had I known that) にも起こることを述べている。

疑問詞はどこに移動するのか？

これまで挙げた疑問文はいずれも **yes-no** 疑問文であったが，最後に，what, who, where などの疑問詞を含む **wh疑問文** について説明しておこう。wh 疑問文では，What will he buy? のように，疑問詞が文頭に移動するが，その移動先は，正確に言うとどのような位置なのだろうか。

図2で，補文標識の位置を C としたが，その上に CP (Complementizer Phrase) という節点を仮定する。

図3

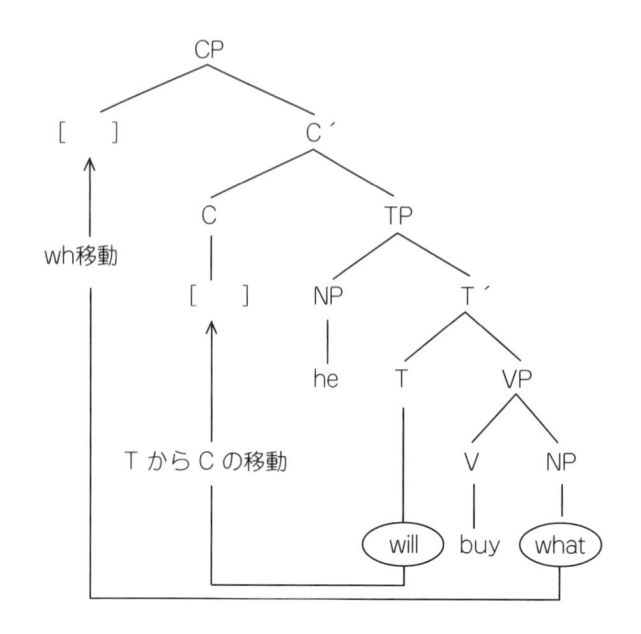

このように，疑問詞は，wh-移動によってCPの先頭（指定部（Specifier）という）へ移動する。このwh-移動は，主節でも従属節でも適用する。

17. a. What will he buy?
    b. I wonder what he will buy.

Comprehension Check

✎ 空所を埋めなさい。

　一見したところ，英語の文は（主語の）NP と（述語の）VP からなっているように見えるが，NP＋VP という式に含まれない要素として高校の英文法でも勉強した（　　　）がある。その要素が VP に属さない証拠として，VP が（　　　）されてもその要素は残るということが挙げられる。もっと一般的に言うと，それに当たる要素が目に見える形で存在しない文でも，NP と VP の間に PRES や PAST という（　　　）の表示を含む抽象的な要素（　　　）があると考えられる。つまり，英語の基本的な文構造は NP＋VP ではなく，（　　）＋（　　）＋（　　）だということになる。さらに，I know that he will come. の that や I wonder if he will come. の if という「接続詞」は補文を導入する役割から（　　　）と呼ばれ，統語構造では（　　　）という節点に位置すると分析される。疑問文を作るときには，助動詞があれば助動詞がその節点に移動し，助動詞がなければ（　　　）が挿入される。wh 疑問文では，さらにその左の方に（　　　）が移動する。（　　　）の要素を平叙文の主要部と分析し，（　　　）の要素を疑問文の主要部と分析することによって，文構造はそれ以外の句構造と同じように，主要部のある構造として統一的に捉えられる。最後に，シェイクスピア時代の英語においては，平叙文では（　　　）だけではなく（　　　）も（　　　）に位置し，疑問文ではそれが（　　　）に移動するということが分かった。

Exercises

(1) まず，a の例文に動詞句削除（VP deletion）を適用してみよう。

　　a.　If you drop out, Sue will drop out, too.

動詞句削除を適用したあとの文を b に書きなさい。

　　b.　(　　　　　　　　　　　　　　　　)

その通り。If you drop out, Sue will, too. となる。なぜなら，you drop out の drop out と，Sue will drop out の drop out が，まったく同じ形であるから，後のほうが消されるわけである。このように，動詞句削除は「同じ形」の動詞句に適用するということが前提となる。そうすると，次の c はどうなるだろうか？

　　c.　Jim dropped out, and Sue will drop out, too.

c に動詞句削除を適用すると，d のようになる。

　　d.　Jim dropped out, and Sue will ~~drop out~~, too.

d では，前半が dropped out という過去形であるのに，後半の削除された部分は

drop out という原形であるから，一見したところ，形が食い違っている。削除されるのは「同じ形」の動詞句であるという前提を維持するためには，d の構造をどのように考えればよいか説明しなさい。

(2) 次の疑問文が，その基になる文から，どのようにして派生(derive)されるか説明しなさい。

    a. Which dictionary can I borrow?
       （基になる文構造：I can borrow which dictionary?）
    b. What did he buy in Shibuya?
       （基になる文構造：He PAST buy what in Shibuya?）

(3) 本文の例(10b)では，if I had known の if の位置に had を移動させる構文を見た。これは文語体の構文だが，自分でも使えるように練習してみよう。次の例文から if を削除して，文章を書き換えなさい。また，当該部分の構造を統語構造で表しなさい。

    a. If you should change your mind, please give me a call.
    b. If he were to give up smoking, she might go out with him.
    c. If he had known that, he wouldn't have bought it.

(4) 英語を習いはじめの生徒は，"Does he like her?" の代わりに "*Does he likes her?" と言ったり，"Did he go?" の代わりに "*Did he went?" と言ったりする。"*Does he likes her?" や "*Did he went?" がなぜ間違いなのかを，T(tense)と do 挿入を用いて説明しなさい。

(5) 本文では，例文(4a)のように助動詞のない文や，例文(2a)，(2b)のように助動詞が 1 つある文を見た。助動詞の数に関しては，ほかにも可能性が 2 つある。つまり，助動詞が 2 つある文および助動詞が 3 つある文も存在するわけである（以下の例文を参照）。

    a. Sue will have written a novel by the end of the year.
    b. Sue may be writing a novel when Jim visits.
    c. Sue has been writing a novel since the beginning of the year.
    d. Sue could have been writing a novel instead of working at McDonald's.

例文 a〜d に見られる助動詞は，(a)進行形の be/been (または am/are/is/was/were)，(b)完了形の have (または has/had)，(c)「法助動詞」(modal auxiliaries) の will/would, can/could, may/might など，という 3 つのタイプに分類することができる。a〜d の例文を参照しながら，その 3 つのタイプの語順を説明しなさい。

(6) 本文で見たように，現代英語の一般動詞は常に V に位置し，T に移動することはない。一方，練習問題(5)で見たことからすると，法助動詞は常に T に位置すると考えることができる。それに対して，完了形の have と 進行形の be の位置は，2 通りの可能性がある。この問題では，完了形の have の位置を調べることとする。

I. 次の例文(1)に動詞句削除を適用すると，(2a)と(2b)の 2 つの文ができ，どちらも英語として適格である。

(1) Sue will have written a novel by the end of the year, and Jim will have written a novel by the end of the year too.

(2) a. Sue will have written a novel by the end of the year, and Jim will have too.
b. Sue will have written a novel by the end of the year, and Jim will too.

設問A. このことを証拠に，ラベルつきの括弧([$_{VP}$])を使って例文(3)における VP の範囲を示しなさい。

(3) Sue will have written a novel by the end of the year.

設問B. (3)における have はどこ(何の節点)に位置するのか，A の解答を証拠に，その位置を書きなさい。

II. 次の例文(4)に動詞句削除を適用すると，(5a)と(5b)の 2 つの文ができ，どちらも英語として適格である。

(4) Sue has been writing a novel since the beginning of the year, and Jim has been writing a novel since the beginning of the year too.

(5) a. Sue has been writing a novel since the beginning of the year, and Jim has been too.
b. Sue has been writing a novel since the beginning of the year, and Jim has too.

設問C. そのことを証拠に，ラベルつきの括弧（[_VP]）を使って例文(6)における VP の範囲を示しなさい。

(6) Sue has been writing a novel since the beginning of the year.

設問D. (6)における have(has)はどこ(何の節点)に位置するのか，C の解答を証拠に，その位置を書きなさい。

Chapter 7　How Sentences Mean: Semantics II

> **BASIC QUESTIONS**
> 単語の意味は辞書に載っているが，文全体の解釈は辞書に載っていない。文全体の意味はどのようにして解釈されるのだろうか。

SEMANTIC ROLES AND ARGUMENT STRUCTURE

In Chapters 5 and 6, we learned how English sentences are constructed. In this chapter, we will learn about various aspects of sentence meaning. To begin with, let us think about how a sentence depends on the properties of its verb.

Any speaker of English will be able to tell you that the sentence *The boys laughed* is grammatical, while **The clown laughed the boys* is not. This is the result of the fact that the verb *laugh* can occur with a subject, but not with an object — alternatively, the fact that it occurs in the SV sentence pattern, but not in the SVO pattern. We may say that for each verb, the possible sentence patterns it can occur in are specified in the native speaker's mental dictionary or lexicon. Verbs with very similar meanings may occur in different sentence patterns. Compare in this regard *break* with *destroy,* and *eat* with *devour*.

(1) a.　The boy broke the window.
　　a´.　The window broke.
　　b.　The boy destroyed the window.
　　b´.　*The window destroyed.
(2) a.　The children ate the sandwiches.
　　a´.　The children ate at eight.
　　b.　The children devoured the sandwiches.
　　b´.　*The children devoured at eight.

In (1), *break* can be used either in the SVO pattern or in the SV pattern, but *destroy* is possible only in the SVO pattern. In (2), similarly, *eat* can be used in either the SVO or the SV pattern, but *devour* allows only SVO. In a word, *destroy* and *devour* are strictly **transitive**, while *break* and *eat* may be either transitive or **intransitive**.

transitive verb = 他動詞
intransitive verb = 自動詞

The traditional distinction between transitive and intransitive verbs, however, is insufficient to understand the data of (1) and (2). In particular, there is an important difference between intransitive *break* and intransitive *eat* that is not brought out by the traditional terminology, namely that they take different kinds of subjects. Note that the subject of intransitive *break* in (1a′) corresponds to the object of transitive *break* in (1a), while the subject of intransitive *eat* in (2a′) corresponds to the subject of transitive *eat* in (2a). Further, reversing this pattern results in ungrammaticality:

(3) a.　*The boy broke.
　　b.　*The sandwiches ate.

terminology＝専門用語

Clearly, specifying the sentence patterns in which a verb occurs requires reference to more than just the distinction between SV and SVO.

Instead of using the terms "subject" and "object," let us refer to the person who performs an action as an **Agent**, and the person or thing which undergoes or is affected by the action as a **Patient**. "Agent" and "Patient" are examples of the **semantic roles** that are played by the **arguments** of a verb, the participants in the action expressed by that verb. The set of semantic roles each verb can take is referred to as the **argument structure** of that verb. For example, the argument structures of the four verbs we saw in (1)-(2) will be as given below:

Agent＝動作主
Patient＝被動者
semantic role＝意味役割
argument＝項

argument structure＝
項構造

Argument structure
● *destroy* and *devour* (always transitive): Agent, Patient
● *break* (either transitive or intransitive): (Agent), Patient
● *eat* (either transitive or intransitive): Agent, (Patient)

With *destroy* and *devour*, both Agent and Patient are **obligatory**, or required. *Break*, on the other hand, can take either a Patient only, as in *The window broke*, or both an Agent and a Patient, as in *The boy broke the window*. With *break*, in other words, while a Patient is obligatory, an Agent is optional — that is, it may be either present or absent. This is indicated above by the placement of *break*'s Agent role in parentheses. Now it is

obligatory＝義務的

parentheses＝丸括弧

possible to see why (3a) is bad: a Patient is obligatory with *break*, but (3a) has only an Agent. Now look at our specification for the argument structure of *eat*, which is the exact opposite of that for *break*. With *eat*, in other words, an Agent is obligatory, but a Patient is optional. *Eat*, then, can take either an Agent only (*The children ate*) or both an Agent and a Patient (*The children ate the sandwiches*). (3b) is ungrammatical because it has only a Patient.

Consider now the interpretations of sentences like *He reached the shore* and *She left the town*. Both of these will be included in the SVO pattern, but that pattern does not tell us how the interpretations of the objects differ in these two sentences. In *He reached the shore,* the object *the shore* is not a Patient (something that undergoes or is affected by the action of the verb). Rather, it may be called a **Goal** because it represents the endpoint of the subject's motion. In contrast, *the town* in *She left the town* may be called a **Source**, because it represents the starting point of the subject's motion. For the verb *leave*, the Source is optional, as you can see from the **grammaticality** of *She left*. The argument structures of *reach* and *leave* may thus be represented as follows:

Goal = 着点

Source = 起点

grammaticality = 文法性

- *reach* : Agent, Goal
- *leave* : Agent, (Source)

Semantic roles are played not only by subjects and direct objects but also by **indirect** and **prepositional objects**. In *He walks to school*, for example, *school* is a Goal. Below we give the argument structures of *hand* and *steal* and example sentences for those verbs:

indirect object = 間接目的語
prepositional object = 前置詞の目的語

- *hand* : Agent, Patient, Goal
    e.g. *He handed the money to Mary.*
    He handed Mary the money.
- *steal* : Agent, Patient, (Source)
    e.g. *He stole the money (from the lady).*

The noun phrases of a sentence, then, are interpreted by referring to the argument structures of the relevant verbs as stored in the native speaker's mental lexicon.

SELECTIONAL RESTRICTIONS

The native speaker's lexicon includes another kind of information that is necessary to interpret sentences. In putting together a phrase or a sentence, it's not possible to combine words with complete freedom. For example, there is a restriction on the set of nouns that can fit in the slot *a pretty _____*. The adjective *pretty* normally goes with a woman or girl, or with a small thing like a flower. Thus, it is strange to say *a pretty man, though you can say *a handsome man*. Semantic conditions of this kind are called **selectional restrictions**.

selectional restriction = 選択制限

Selectional restrictions hold not only for combinations of adjectives and nouns but also for combinations of verbs and objects/subjects, or verbs and adverbs. Let us consider *grow, raise,* and *bring up*, all meaning「育てる」. Which verb can occur with which object?

(object nouns)	three children	beard	vegetables	cattle
grow (tr.)	*	OK	OK	*
raise	OK	?	OK	OK
bring up	OK	*	*	*

In the table, OK indicates acceptable combinations, and the asterisk (*) shows incompatibility. For example, we can say *He grows vegetables in the garden*, but not **He grew three children*. On the other hand, we can say *He brought up three children*, but not **He brought up vegetables*. When the object is a human noun like *children*, both *raise* and *bring up* are good, but *grow* is not suitable. Note, however, that when used as an intransitive verb, *grow* is free from such restrictions and can be applied to any of *children, beard, vegetables,* and *cattle*.

CONSTRUCTIONAL MEANING

In English, when a direct object is replaced by a prepositional phrase, the meaning sometimes changes in a semi-systematic way.

(4) a. He kicked <u>the dog</u>. (His leg reached the dog.)
    b. He kicked <u>at the dog</u>. (He tried to kick the dog, but it is not clear whether his leg reached it.)
(5) a. She climbed <u>the mountain</u>. (She walked up the mountain to the top.)
    b. She climbed <u>up the mountain</u>. (She walked up the mountain, but it is not clear whether she got to the top.)

In (4a), the subject completed his kick, and in (5a), the subject completed her climb. (4b) and (5b), in contrast, do not entail such completion of action.

A similar difference is found in pairs that exemplify the **locative alternation**, as in (6).

locative alternation = 場所格交替

(6) a. He sprayed paint <u>on the wall</u>. (It is not clear whether he painted the whole wall or only a part of it.)
    b. He sprayed <u>the wall</u> with paint. (Most likely, the entire wall was painted.)

In (6a), where *the wall* is the object of the preposition *on*, the proportion of the wall that was painted is left vague. In contrast, (6b), where *the wall* is the direct object, strongly suggests that the entire wall was painted.

In the case of the **dative alternation** (already illustrated above with the verb *hand*), a different distinction between direct and prepositional objects is observed:

dative alternation = 与格交替

(7) a. Sue sent a package <u>to Jim</u>.
    b. Sue sent <u>Jim</u> a package.

(7b) does show a slight increase, compared with (7a), in the degree to which the action of sending is felt to be likely to have been completed in the sense that the package reaches Jim. As the acceptability of *Sue sent Jim a package, but he never got it* shows, however, this is only a weak tendency. A clearer difference between the **dative construction** of (7a) and the **double object construction** of (7b) is that the first ("indirect") object of the double object construction must be the intended recipient of the second ("direct") object. Thus, *Sue sent a package to New York* is acceptable, but **Sue sent New York a package* is not: New

acceptability = 容許性

dative construction = 与格構文
double object construction = 二重目的語構文
recipient = 受け取り手

York, being inanimate, cannot be the intended recipient of a package.

To this point, we have been comparing direct/indirect and prepositional objects. A difference similar to the ones we have observed can be seen in the contrast between the meaning of verbs of perception used with (a) object plus verb complements and (b) full sentential complements:

(8) a. I heard the dog bark.
    b. I hear that the dog barks every night.
(9) a. They looked for the man and found him dead in the woods.
    b. Looking at the newspaper, they found that the man had been dead for several days.

The verbs *hear* and *find* in (8a) and (9a) mean that the subjects perceived the objects directly, but the same verbs in (8b) and (9b) have lost the sense of physical perception and mean 'learn a fact indirectly'.

WORD ORDER AND INFORMATION

Besides the basic word orders illustrated by the "five sentence patterns," English has many "non-basic" patterns in which the order of words is changed. Change of word order brings about a change in emphasis. For example, the basic SVO pattern is changed into OSV by moving an object to the beginning of the sentence. This is called **topicalization**.

● **Topicalization**: John likes wine.→**Wine,** John likes (but not beer).

The moved or topicalized element, *wine,* is pronounced with a falling-rising intonation. From the point of view of meaning, the topicalized element in such a sentence is **old information** (it has typically been introduced into the conversation earlier) and is implicitly or explicitly contrasted with something else — in the case at hand, beer.

Just as topicalization results in the placement of old information at the beginning of the sentence, there is a general tendency to put an element that is important in the sense of being **new**

information at the end. This is called the **Principle of End Focus**. In passive sentences like *The boy was bitten by this dog*, the Prepositional Phrase *by this dog* that expresses the Agent is the **focus** of the sentence. This explains why we don't use *by them* when we make the passive sentence *Spanish is spoken in Mexico* from the active sentence *They speak Spanish in Mexico*.

- **Passive**: They speak Spanish in Mexico.→Spanish is spoken in Mexico.

The pronoun *they,* here meaning 'people in Mexico', is nonspecific and cannot be the focus of the passive sentence.

Taking advantage of the Principle of End Focus, English has special **transformations** that move a long and important phrase to the end of a sentence. See how the "top-heavy" sentences are transformed into "bottom-heavy" ones in the following examples.

- **Extraposition**
  Where he has gone is not known.
  →It is not known where he has gone.
- **Extraposition from NP**
  A report that the suspect was arrested has just been received.
  →A report has just been received that the suspect was arrested.
- **Inversion**
  The fact that the President lied in court is particularly important.
  →Particularly important is the fact that the President lied in court.
- **Heavy NP Shift**
  I will regard anyone who can solve this problem as a genius.
  →I will regard as a genius anyone who can solve this problem.

It should be noted that these special transformations tend to be limited to written English or formal style.

WHAT DO PRONOUNS REFER TO?

English pronouns referring to human beings can be divided into two types: ordinary **personal pronouns** (*he, his, him,* etc.) and **reflexive pronouns** (*himself, herself,* etc.). How are these two types of pronouns interpreted in context?

(10) Jack criticized himself. (himself=Jack)
(11) Jack criticized him. (him ≠ Jack)

Sentence (10) is easy to understand. The reflexive pronoun *himself* can refer only to the same person as the subject NP *Jack; Jack,* in other words, is the **antecedent** of the pronoun. More generally, an English reflexive pronoun and its antecedent must be within the same simple sentence. In a complex sentence like (12), *himself* cannot refer to the subject *Jack* in the main clause.

(12)　*Jack thought that Mary criticized *himself.*

This is because *Jack* and *himself* belong to different clauses.

What about example (11)? Unlike *himself*, the personal pronoun *him* in (11) cannot refer to the same person as the subject *Jack* but instead is understood as referring to someone else who has been discussed in the conversation. This shows that a personal pronoun and its antecedent must NOT occur within the same simple sentence. From these observations we can predict that if *himself* in example (12) is replaced by *him*, that pronoun should be able to refer to Jack. This prediction is correct.

(13)　Jack thought that Mary criticized *him*.

(Note that in (13), *him* may also refer to someone else who is under discussion.)

To summarize the preceding discussion, we have the following rules for the interpretation of *himself* and *him*.

　Condition A:　A reflexive pronoun and its antecedent must occur within the same simple sentence.
　Condition B:　A personal pronoun and its antecedent must not occur within the same simple sentence.

Our formulation of Conditions A and B raises the question of what exactly "the same simple sentence" means. There is no question, first of all, that (14) and (15), like (10) and (11), are simple sentences, so we predict correctly that the reflexive pronouns can refer to the underlined NPs.

(14)　Sue talked to Bill about *herself*.
(15)　Sue talked to Bill about *himself*.

antecedent = 先行詞

simple sentence = 単文

Now look at (16) and (17), which do raise a question about the meaning of "simple sentence."

(16) *<u>John</u> believes [_{CP} that *himself* is a genius].
(17) <u>John</u> believes [_{TP} *himself* to be a genius].

In (16), *himself* cannot refer to *John*. This is because the reflexive pronoun and its antecedent, being separated by the complementizer *that*, are not within a "simple sentence." More precisely, (16) is bad because *himself* and *John* are separated by a CP boundary, which marks the boundary of a full clause. In contrast, the sentence in (17) is acceptable with *himself* referring to John. Although *himself to be a genius* is a clause, it is a TP, not a CP. On this basis, we may revise Condition A as follows:

CP→第 6 章を参照

TP→第 6 章を参照

Condition A′: A reflexive pronoun and its antecedent cannot be separated by a CP boundary.

Finally, let us think about personal pronouns in (16) and (17). If *himself* in (16) is replaced by *he*, the sentence becomes acceptable; if *himself* in (17) is replaced by *him*, the sentence becomes unacceptable in the meaning of (17). Condition B, then, may be revised as follows:

Condition B′: A personal pronoun and its antecedent must be separated by (at least one) CP boundary.

An important point about Conditions A′ and B′, suggested already by our first formulation of them above, is that English personal pronouns and reflexive pronouns, to a good first approximation, occur in "complementary" or non-overlapping environments.

complementary＝相補的

Comprehension Check

✎ 空所を埋めなさい。

　　文を作るときにどのような文型を使うかは，動詞に依存する。ある動詞がどのような主語と，どのような目的語を取るかは（　　　）構造に記載されている。destroy は（　　　）と（　　　）が絶対に必要なので，純粋に（　　　）動詞であるが，break は（　　　）があってもなくてもよく，（　　　）だけの場合は（　　　）動詞になる。また，（　　　）と呼ばれる，語と語を結びつけるための意味制約もある。たとえば，同じ「育てる」でも，bring up の目的語は（　　　）に限られ，grow の目的語は（　　　）や（　　　）に限られる。英語では，（　　　）の原則と言われるように，文で最も重要な要素が最後に置かれる傾向がある。この効果を利用して長い表現を文末に移動する（　　　）が幾つかある。

Exercises

(1) 各組の例文において下線部が Agent, Patient, Goal のうちどの意味役割に該当するか示し，それに基づいて，各組で使われている動詞の項構造を示しなさい。[注：与えられた例文についてだけで考える。*印は英語として非文法的，無印は文法的]

1. a. <u>Someone</u> damaged <u>the mechanism</u>.
   b. *<u>The mechanism</u> damaged.
   c. *<u>Someone</u> damaged.

2. a. <u>The boy</u> shattered <u>the plate</u>.
   b. <u>The plate</u> shattered.
   c. *<u>The boy</u> shattered.

3. a. <u>Mother</u> put <u>the dishes</u> on <u>the table</u>.
   b. *<u>Mother</u> put <u>the dishes</u>.
   c. *<u>Mother</u> put on <u>the table</u>.
   d. *<u>Mother</u> put.

4. a. <u>The students</u> entered <u>the room</u>.
   b. <u>The students</u> entered.
   c. *<u>The room</u> entered.

5. a. <u>John</u> sent <u>the letter</u> to <u>the wrong address</u>.
   b. <u>John</u> sent <u>the letter</u>.
   c. *<u>John</u> sent to <u>the wrong address</u>.

(2) 次の下線部は，本文で述べた意味役割に適合するだろうか？　もしうまく適合しない場合は，どのような名前をつければよいだろうか？

    a. This house is built of <u>brick</u>.
    b. The train is approaching <u>the station</u>.
    c. <u>The bright sunshine</u> hurt her eyes.
    d. She cooked a special dinner for <u>her husband</u>.

(3) インターネットで例を探してみよう。

　英語と日本語で似たような意味の単語でも，選択制限が異なることがある。日本語の「ハンサムな」という表現は男性に限られる（ハンサムなお兄さん／＊ハンサムなお姉さん）が，英語の handsome の使い方はどうだろうか。また，日本語の「登る」は「上方向に」限られる（上に登る／＊下に登る）が，英語の climb はどのような前置詞と一緒に使うことができるだろうか。

　実際にどのような組み合わせが可能か，インターネットのコーパスを使って調べてみよう（コーパス（corpus）とは，小説や新聞など大量の資料を集めて機械的に処理できるようにしたもの）。次のサイトで，大型コーパスを無料で試すことができる。

    Corpus of Contemporary American English
    http://corpus.byu.edu/coca/

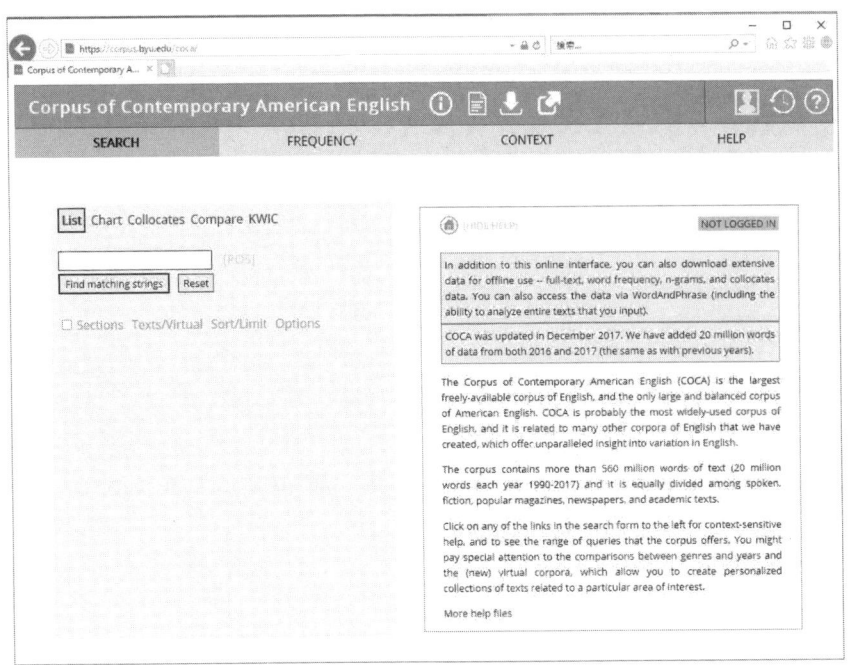

British National Corpus (BYU-BNC)
http://corpus.byu.edu/bnc/

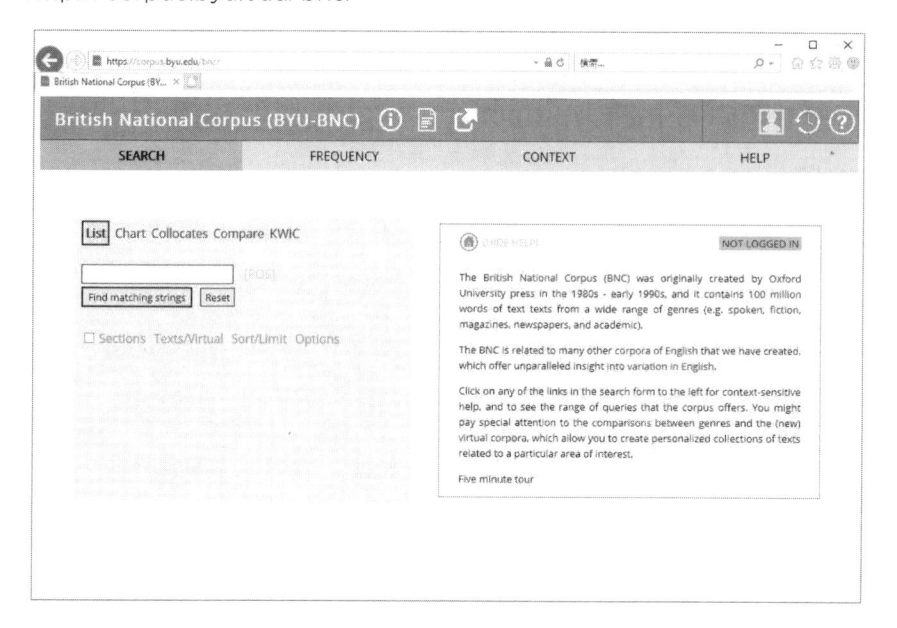

それぞれのページを開くと，検索ウィンドウが出てくる。そこに handsome と入力すると，限られた数ではあるが，実例が出てくるから，handsome が使われている部分を抜き出して，選択制限を調べなさい。同じように，climb を入力して，どのような例文が出てくるか試してみなさい。更に，たとえば a handsome と入力すると，次に来る名詞がよりはっきりする。

(4) 次の例文は一見したところ意味が取りにくいが，強いて解釈するとどのような意味になるだろうか。また，その意味解釈はどのようにして得られるのだろうか。

　　a. She read the building.
　　b. He broke the dog.
　　c. She was wearing a towel.
　　d. He paid three stones for the car.

(5) 下線部の前置詞の有無に注意しながら，各組の意味の違いを述べなさい。

1.　a. He shot at the lion.
　　b. He shot the lion.

2. a. She swam <u>in the lake</u>.
   b. She swam <u>the lake</u>.
3. a. He sprinkled water <u>on the lawn</u>.
   b. He sprinkled <u>the lawn</u> with water.

(6) 示された変形を用いて，下線部が文末に来るように書き換えなさい。また，書き換えの前と後とで，意味（情報伝達）がどのように異なるか説明しなさい。

　　a. <u>A world-famous architect</u> designed the new school building.（Passive）
　　b. <u>The price of meat</u> went up and up.（Inversion）
　　c. <u>How easily children learn to talk</u> is quite surprising.（Extraposition）
　　d. A sudden fear <u>that someone was following her</u> seized the girl.
　　　（Extraposition from NP）
　　e. I showed <u>all the letters I had received from my former girlfriend</u> to my wife.
　　　（Heavy NP Shift）

(7) 人称代名詞および再帰代名詞が下線部の名詞を指すと解釈できる場合には○，そのように解釈できない場合には×をつけなさい。

　　a. (　　) <u>Mary</u> looked at *herself* in the mirror.
　　b. (　　) <u>Bill</u> wonders if John hates *himself*.
　　c. (　　) <u>Bill</u> regards *himself* as a genius.
　　d. (　　) <u>Bill</u> thought *him* to be a genius.
　　e. (　　) <u>Bill and Tom</u> threw snowballs at *them*.

Chapter 8 How to Communicate with Other People: Pragmatics

> **BASIC QUESTIONS**
> これまでの章では，人間の脳の中にある文法について学んだが，ことばというものは，人と人のあいだで使われて初めてコミュニケーションの機能をはたす。人と人との会話はどのようにして成り立っているのだろうか。英語には「敬語」のようなものがないのだろうか。

WHAT IS PRAGMATICS?

While semantics (Chapters 4 and 7) is concerned with native speakers' internalized knowledge of meaning, pragmatics, the topic of this chapter, deals with the external relations between people who talk with each other.

conversation＝会話

In order to build good interpersonal relations, people must be considerate to each other not only in their physical behavior but also in the language they use.

FORMAL VS. INFORMAL STYLE

Just as in Japanese we change our linguistic style depending on who we are talking to and on what occasion, so speakers of English choose, consciously or unconsciously, the most appropriate style for the situation they are in. The linguist Martin Joos once distinguished five different **styles**: (a) **frozen style** (the most formal style limited to ceremonies or dignified speeches and writings), (b) **formal style** (used on business and other formal occasions or in formal letters), (c) **consultative style** (ordinary colloquial conversation with no formality), (d) **casual style** (informal conversation between friends), and (e) **intimate style** (between two people of intimate relations such as husband and wife). It is recommended that foreign learners of English be able to distinguish the three styles in the middle, that is, (b), (c), and

formal＝改まった
informal＝くだけた，格式ばらない
style＝スタイル（文体），スピーチレベルとも言う

frozen style＝
凍結スタイル
formal style＝
正式スタイル
consultative style＝
協議スタイル
casual style＝
略式スタイル
intimate style＝
親密スタイル

(d). These three styles will be illustrated with the following greetings between two people who are meeting for the first time.

(b) Formal style:
[Smith] *How do you do, Mr. Johnson.*
[Johnson] *How do you do, Mr. Smith.*
(c) Consultative style:
[Bill] *Nice to meet you, Fred.*
[Fred] *Nice to meet you, Bill.*
(d) Casual style:
[Bill] *Hi, Fred.*
[Fred] *Hi, Bill.*

If you choose the wrong style, you may get a strange or chilly look.

POLITENESS

politeness = ポライトネス，丁寧さ

convey = 伝える
interlocutor = 対話者

Perhaps the most important thing in conversation is that your message is conveyed to your interlocutor — that is, the person you are talking to — just as you intended and without offending him or her. The explanation of how the message is conveyed is put off until the next section; this section explains how not to offend your interlocutor. Consider the following four **imperative sentences**.

imperative sentence = 命令文

(1) Lend me $100.
(2) Pass the salt.
(3) Help yourself to the cake.
(4) Have a nice day.

abrupt = 無愛想な

All of these are grammatical sentences, but (1) and (2) would sound rude or abrupt if used just as they are in actual conversation. In such a case, *would/could you (please)*, *Do you think you could*, or some similar expression must be added at the beginning (*Would you please pass the salt?*, *Do you think you could pass the salt?*). On the other hand, (3) and (4) are not rude even though each takes the imperative form. In fact, it would be very strange to add *would/could you(please)* to (3) and (4). Why is there such a difference between (1)-(2) and (3)-(4)?

The sentences in (1) and (2) express the speaker's desire; the speaker wants the hearer to do a favor for him or her. The speaker's request is fulfilled at some expense to the hearer, and only the speaker benefits from the hearer's action. In such a situation, the speaker must be careful to reduce the hearer's burden as much as possible. One way to do this, of course, is to reduce the size of the request itself (*Lend me $10* instead of *Lend me $100*), but another way is to lighten the hearer's mental burden by using a polite marker like *could you*. In contrast, the suggested actions in (3) and (4) bring benefit to the hearer rather than to the speaker. Because the requested actions are not costly for the hearer at all, *would/could you* is not necessary, and these "imperative" sentences are interpreted as offers or recommendations rather than requests or demands.

The essence of such interpersonal interactions is captured in Geoffrey Leech's **Tact Maxim**: "Minimize the cost to other; maximize the benefit to other." The tact maxim will enable us to understand why questions with *will/would* and *can/could* make the request polite. *Will* and *would* convey the subject's willingness to perform an action, and *can* and *could* the subject's ability to perform an action. Thus, in uttering the sentence *Would/Could you bring me the coffee?* the speaker tries to decrease the hearer's cost by asking whether he or she is willing or able to perform the action. In other words, the polite questions in principle give the hearer the option of declining to carry out the speaker's request.

Now why is it that the past forms *would* and *could* are more polite than the present forms *will* and *can*? One way of explaining this is to say that the past forms actually do not represent the "past" tense but the **subjunctive mood**, used to express a hypothetical situation. A hypothetical request (essentially "Suppose I were to ask you") is easier for the hearer to refuse than a direct and urgent request that uses the present tense or **indicative mood**.

In many cases, the directness of a request is closely related to the social or psychological distance between the speaker and the hearer. When you speak to someone who is much higher in rank and hence socially as well as psychologically distant from you, you will most likely use a long expression like *Could you lend me your eraser?* or *Would it be possible for me to use your eraser?* In this case you show deference by preserving the other's **negative face**. Negative face, in Brown and Levinson's theory of politeness, refers to our need to be independent and not to be disturbed by or imposed on by others. The other side of face is **positive face**, which refers to our need to be liked by others and accepted as a member of a social group. Use of nicknames, **colloquial ellipsis**, and other expressions of informal style serve to show solidarity and preserve positive face. If you want to borrow an eraser from a close friend, you will probably make use of positive politeness with such informal expressions like *Do you have an eraser I can use?* or *Got an eraser?* Between friends, in other words, the more informal way of speaking is actually more "polite." Imagine how your friend would react if you said, *Mr. Thomas, would you mind if I borrowed your eraser?* Viewed in this light, politeness is not just a matter of language but concerns the consideration you show to others in order to make interpersonal relations flow more smoothly.

SPEECH ACTS CD Track 16

What a sentence conveys does not always correspond to what you might expect on the basis of its syntactic form. We already saw such a case in (3) and (4), where the "imperative" construction conveys an offer or recommendation rather than an order. Likewise, *Could you pass the salt?* has the form of a question but is really a request. It is thus necessary to distinguish between the form of a sentence and the meaning it actually conveys.

From one point of view, the three basic sentence types are declaratives, interrogatives (questions), and imperatives, which normally perform the following (**direct**) **speech acts**:

Sentence Type	declarative	interrogative	imperative
Speech Act	conveying information	asking for information	requesting action

In the table above, each of the three sentence types corresponds directly to a particular speech act. In actuality, however, there is almost an endless number of actions that we perform with words, including thanking, promising, threatening, offering, reprimanding, accusing, insulting, apologizing, and encouraging. The three sentence types in their basic meanings above do not cover all of these and must be extended to "non-literal" meanings. For example, *Could you pass the salt?*, in its **literal meaning**, is a question asking the hearer's ability, but the same sentence is more commonly interpreted in the non-literal meaning of making a request. When a teacher says to her student, "You're late!" she is scolding him; when a bank robber says, "I've got a gun!" he is making a threat; and when a doctor says to a nurse, "I need a scalpel," he is making a request. In these examples, scolding, threatening, and requesting are performed indirectly by declarative sentences, whose most basic function is simply to convey information. Derived speech acts of this kind are called **indirect speech acts**.

non-literal =
文字通りでない
literal meaning =
文字通りの意味

indirect speech act =
間接発話行為

CONVERSATIONAL IMPLICATURE (CD) Track 17

An angry father says to his daughter who has come home after midnight, "Do you know what time it is?" Is he really asking her the time? If the daughter answers her father, "Let me see. It's 12:15," will he be satisfied? No, he isn't asking her the time (which he is well aware of). In such a context, the question "Do you know what time it is?" serves as an indirect speech act of scolding and conveys the anger of the speaker. (The intonation of the question is also typically different in such a context from when it is used as a request for information.) This kind of indirectly understood meaning is called a **conversational implicature**.

It is very important to distinguish conversational implicatures

intonation =
イントネーション，音調
（文における声の上がり下がり）
context = 文脈，場面
conversational implicature
= 会話の含意

from "entailments." As explained in Chapter 4, entailments constitute part of the linguistic meaning of words and sentences. For example, as we saw in Chapter 4, the sentence *The boy drowned in the river* entails that the boy died. It is contradictory to say **The boy drowned in the river, but he's still alive*. Entailments, in other words, cannot be **canceled**. In contrast, a conversational implicature is cancelable. The angry father in the above story might add, "But I'm not scolding you. I was just worried about you."

Below we see a few more examples of conversational implicature.

(5) *Husband* : Is there anything I can do?
Wife : The garbage isn't out yet.
(6) *You* : How do you like that singer's new CD?
Friend : Well, the jacket's pretty cool.

The wife's statement in (5) probably means that she wants her husband to take the garbage out, and the friend's answer in (6), which will be discussed further below, is naturally taken as a negative evaluation of the CD.

THE CO-OPERATIVE PRINCIPLE

So far we have found that an utterance typically conveys not only a literal meaning but also an indirect or implied meaning. The question of how we infer these indirect meanings is an interesting one, partly because, at least for the present, only human beings (and not computers) can understand them.

The answer proposed by the philosopher Paul Grice is that human beings are able to make inferences based on the **Co-operative Principle**. This principle is made up of four parts:

Co-operative Principle
1. **Maxim of quantity**: Make your contribution as informative as is required. Do not make your contribution more informative than is required.
2. **Maxim of quality**: Do not say what you believe to be false. Do not say that for which you lack adequate evidence.
3. **Maxim of relation**: Be relevant.
4. **Maxim of manner**: Avoid obscurity of expression. Avoid ambiguity. Be brief. Be orderly.

All these maxims state commonsense regulations which people are normally assumed to obey in using language. But if everyone always observed these maxims rigidly, language would be somewhat stiff and uninteresting. Human beings are capable of creating new, non-literal meanings by intentionally violating one or more of the above maxims.

intentionally＝意図的に
violate＝違反する

Let us consider again the mini-dialogue of (6), repeated below. How do you understand your friend's conversational implicature?

(6) *You*: How do you like that singer's new CD?
　　Friend: Well, the jacket's pretty cool.

You ask your friend for her evaluation of the new CD, and the answer begins with *Well*. Since the **interjection** *well* is a marker of hesitation, you might infer immediately that your friend was not very enthusiastic about the CD. Next, the sentence *the jacket's pretty cool* mentions only a relatively minor aspect of the CD album. Here, your friend observes the maxim of relation, because the **definite article** (*the*) indicates that *the jacket* referred to is that of the CD. The maxims of manner and quality are also observed. But your friend seems to be intentionally violating the maxim of quantity, since she says nothing about the music, presumably the most important aspect of the CD. You thus arrive at the conclusion that your friend had a low opinion of the music.

interjection＝間投詞

definite article＝定冠詞

This example shows how important it is to "read between the lines" in conversation as well as in reading. A sentence may convey many more things than its literal meaning, and those inferred meanings are understood by virtue of the "calculations" that the speaker and hearer make on the basis of the Cooperative Principle and other such rules. As already indicated, such calculations are beyond the ability of present-day computers, even though in other respects a good deal of progress has been made in computer understanding of language.

read between the lines＝
行間を読む

calculation＝計算，推定

Comprehension Check

✎ 空所を埋めなさい。

　　ことばには改まった言い方とくだけた言い方のような（　　　）の区別があり，相手や状況に応じて使い分ける必要がある。日本語の「～です」とか「～します」といった丁寧語の形式は英語にはないが，しかし英語でも丁寧か失礼かという感覚は当然ある。それは，一言でいうと，「（　　　）を最小化し，（　　　）を最大化しなさい」という思いやりのことである。Have a nice day. のように相手の利益を述べるときには，（　　　）文であっても失礼ではない。他方，Lend me $100. のように（　　　）を述べるときには，（　　　）や（　　　）などの言葉を付け加えなければ無礼なことになる。基本的には，平叙文は「断定」，疑問文は「質問」のように文型と意味が対応しているが，現実には疑問文が（　　　）を表したり，（　　　）を表したりする。このように，文型が本来，表す以外の意味機能を果たすことを（　　　）と言う。ことばには，文字通りの意味と，それが使われる文脈から生じる間接的な意味がある。前者は論理的（　　　），後者は（　　　）と呼ばれ，前者は「取り消し」がきかないが，後者は取り消すことができる。このような間接的な意味を察知することは，グライスの（　　　）によって可能になる。

Exercises

(1) 次の各組は，(a)＞(b)＞(c)または(a)＞(b)の順で，改まったスタイルからくだけたスタイルに並んでいる。それぞれのスタイルに合うように，適切な英語を補いなさい。

I. あなたが，Tom Cooper という人を Jane Hill という人に紹介する。

(a) You: (　　　), may I (　　　) you to Mr. Cooper of XYZ Company?

(b) You: Jane, (　　　) Tom Cooper.

(c) You: (　　　), this is (　　　).

II. 手紙を書くとき，結びのことば(complimentary close)。

(a) 結び：

(b) 結び：Best wishes,

(c) 結び：

III. お礼を言うとき。

(a)

(b)

IV. お礼を言われたとき,「どういたしまして」と答える。
(a)
(b) Don't mention it.
(c)

(2) 1〜6 の英語を,最も直接的な命令から丁寧な依頼まで,順番に並べ替えなさい。また,なぜその順番になるのかを説明しなさい。

1. Would you take this chair out of the room?
2. Can you take this chair out of the room?
3. Take this chair out of the room.
4. Will you take this chair out of the room?
5. Would you mind taking this chair out of the room?
6. Could you take this chair out of the room?

(3) 各組において,a と b のどちらが「丁寧」だろうか。理由も説明しなさい。

1. 親しい友達に飲み物を勧めるとき。
    a. Something to drink, Sally?
    b. Would you care for a drink, Miss White?
2. パーティに来ているお客さんに食事の後かたづけを手伝ってもらう。
    a. Wash the dishes, will you?
    b. I have so many things to do. Can I ask you to help me wash the dishes?

(4) 次の英文の間接発話行為を説明しなさい。

a. [father to child] You'd better clean up right away.
b. [hostess to guest] You must eat some of this cake I baked.
c. [answering a question] How should I know?
d. [to your friend who looks pale]
   You might want to see a doctor.
e. [policeman to a man who is trying to peep into a girl's room]
   What are you doing there?

(5) Grice の「会話の協調原則」を構成する 4 つの公理とはどのようなものか，日本語で説明しなさい。また，それぞれの公理に反する状況を英語または日本語で考えてみなさい。

(6) a と b のそれぞれの質問に対して，[　]内の意味を伝えたいとき，そのままストレートに言わずに，会話の含意として間接的に表現する文章を英語で作文しなさい

　　a. Can you come to my apartment tonight?　［No, I can't.］
　　b. How was your English exam?　［I didn't do well.］

(7) 次の会話において，B の発言はどういう意味（会話の含意）に解釈できるか。また，なぜそういう含意が生じるのか。会話の協調原則を参照して説明しなさい。

1. A: Pat, will you marry me?
   B: We've always been good friends, haven't we?
2. (The telephone rings.)
   A: Steve, will you get it?
   B: I'm in the bathroom!

言葉にならない言葉

　言語学は言語の形と意味を研究するのが本来であるが，語用論では，言葉にならない言葉も研究の対象となる。言葉にならない言葉というのは，要するに，文字や発音として表されない部分である。俗に言う「行間を読む」とか「言外の意味」というのがそれに当たるが，もう少し広い観点から言えば，「言葉を発しない」つまり「無言」にも意味があるということである。たとえば，質問をされて黙っていると，「分からない，知らない」という意味に取られるだろう。アメリカ人にとっては，いつも声を出してしゃべっているのが，相手に対して「丁寧」である。なぜなら，しゃべるということによって，相手を無視していない，相手の存在を尊重しているということを表すからである。日本人なら，むしろ逆に，「おしゃべり」はよくないので，特に目上の人の前ではおとなしく黙っているほうが礼儀正しいと考えられるだろう。無言が，どのような状況でどのような意味になるか ―「無言の言語学」というのも，考えてみるとおもしろいだろう。

Chapter 9　The Sounds of English: Phonetics and Phonology

> **BASIC QUESTIONS**
> 英語の発音というと，"l" と "r" の区別や，「ア」にもいろいろな種類があるといった，日本語との違いを思い浮かべる。日本人の立場から，英語らしい英語の発音ができるようになるには，どのような点に注意すればよいのだろうか。

SOUND AND MEANING　Track 18

Language can be thought of as a device for connecting sound and meaning. At the level of the word, the sound-meaning connection is notoriously **arbitrary** and unsystematic. For example, there is no necessary connection between the sounds [kæt] or [neko] and the furry four-footed animal to which they both refer. Nor is it generally the case that individual vowels or consonants or sequences thereof have consistent meanings. Intonation, the distribution of high and low **pitches** in a sentence, is a partial exception to this rule, though, since particular sequences of pitches do tend to be associated with relatively stable, identifiable meanings. Let us start this chapter about the sounds of English with a look at one of the most basic meanings conveyed by intonation, the distinction between statements and questions.

arbitrary＝恣意的

pitch＝ピッチ，音の高さ

INTONATION　Track 19

As you already know, statements (declarative sentences) end with a **falling intonation** in English (and many other languages), and questions (interrogative sentences) that can be answered with "yes" or "no" end with a **rising intonation**:

(1) a.　Linguistics is easy.
　　　　(statement: the pitch of *easy* drops from High to Low.)
　　b.　Is linguistics easy?
　　　　(question: the pitch of *easy* rises from Low to High.)

There is also, of course, a word-order difference between the statement and the question. As we saw in Chapter 6, this is due to the fact that in questions, auxiliaries and the copula *be* undergo inversion. Let us see what happens when we combine the rising

statement＝陳述文
falling intonation＝
下降音調
interrogative sentence＝
疑問文
rising intonation＝
上昇音調

intonation characteristic of questions with the basic, non-inverted word order characteristic of statements, and the falling intonation characteristic of statements with the inverted word order characteristic of questions. Will it be the intonation or the word order that determines how the sentence is interpreted?

(2) a. Linguistics is easy?   (question: Low-High)
    b. Is linguistics easy!   (exclamation: High-Low)

In fact, it is the intonation that wins. (2a), with rising intonation, is interpreted as a question (or as an expression of disbelief). (2b), on the other hand, is an exclamation — like an ordinary statement, declarative rather than interrogative. It is clear, then, that intonation is an extremely important aspect of language. In general, falling intonation tends to signal certainty and definiteness, whereas rising intonation is associated with indirect speech acts like asking for approval or confirmation.

WORD ACCENT AND SYLLABLE STRUCTURE CD Track 20

While intonation refers to the rise and fall of pitch in sentence-sized stretches of speech, **accent** refers to relations of **prominence** in words and phrases. The two are connected in that the pitch **peaks** or **troughs** (high or low points) of intonation patterns are aligned with (coincide with) the accented or prominent **syllables** of words or phrases. Remember in this connection that in Chapter 3 we looked at the difference between compound stress and phrasal stress (where stress, as we will see below, is one kind of accent). We noted that the English Compound Stress Rule applies to (compound) words, while the Phrasal Stress Rule applies to phrases.

In the last paragraph, we talked about accented syllables. The term syllable is notoriously difficult to define, but we may consider a syllable to be a sequence of **segments** (vowels or consonants) centered around a "peak," usually a vowel, that is the most **sonorous** (loudest) segment of the sequence. Another way to think about a syllable is as a possible location for accent. Let

exclamation＝感嘆文

indirect speech act→第8章参照

accent＝アクセント
prominence＝際立ち

peak＝山，頂点
trough＝谷，くぼみ
syllable＝音節

segment＝分節音

sonorous＝
聞こえ度(sonority)の大きい

us then consider the topic of word accent. It is instructive to compare and contrast English and Japanese in this respect. Note, to begin with, that both English and Japanese distinguish, among two-syllable words, between those accented on the first syllable and those accented on the second:

(3) a. cónvert_N　転向者
　　b. convért_V　転換する

(4) a. káki（High-Low）牡蛎
　　b. kakí（Low-High）垣

A second similarity is that in both languages, accent is manifested by a fall in pitch from high to low. Thus in both (3a) and (4a), the first syllable is pronounced on a relatively high pitch and the second on a relatively low pitch.

In (3b) and (4b), on the other hand, a difference between English and Japanese appears. In (3b), the high and low pitches associated with the accent appear on the same syllable, and the result is a falling pitch **contour** within the accented syllable. In (4b), on the other hand, the low pitch associated with the accent only appears if something immediately follows the accented syllable, as in *kakí ga* 垣が, with a low-high-low pitch pattern. A further difference between English and Japanese is that while some syllable of an English **content word** (noun, verb, or adjective) must always be accented, Japanese has accentless content words. Thus *kaki* 柿 is unaccented, as shown by the pitch pattern of *kaki ga* 柿が, which is low-high-high.

contour＝音調曲線

content word＝実質語

We have looked at various similarities and differences between English and Japanese accent, but we have not yet touched on what is probably the biggest difference between them, usually described by saying that whereas Japanese has "pitch accent," English has "stress accent." If you say the words of (4) to yourself, you will notice that while your voice goes up or down depending on where the accent is, no syllable can be described as "stronger" than any other, and, crucially, the vowels themselves do not change depending on where the accent falls. In English, in

pitch accent＝
高さアクセント
stress accent＝
強勢アクセント

contrast, stressed syllables are pronounced more strongly than unstressed syllables. The most concrete result of this difference in strength is that the vowels of unstressed syllables, like the first syllable of (3b) above, are "reduced" to the neutral vowel **schwa**, written [ə]. The two related words in (5), where the **acute accent** (´) marks **primary** (strongest) **stress** and the **grave accent** (`) marks **secondary** (next strongest) **stress**, are a good illustration of the reduction of unstressed vowels to schwa.

schwa＝曖昧母音
acute accent＝
鋭アクセント
primary stress＝第一強勢
grave accent＝
重アクセント
secondary stress＝
第二強勢
[ɹ]は英語の r の IPA 表記。IPA 表記については p.109 参照。

(5) a. photograph [fówtəɡɹæ̀f]
    b. photographer [fətɑ́ɡɹəfəɹ]

Note that the stressed syllables of (5a) are both unstressed in (5b), and that their vowels therefore reduce to schwa. Similarly, the stressed vowel of (5b) is unstressed and reduced in (5a).

Another major difference between Japanese and English, related to the fact that Japanese has pitch accent and English has stress accent, is often described by saying that whereas Japanese is **mora-timed** (where a **mora** is equivalent to one *hiragana* or *katakana* character), English is **stress-timed**. Japanese being mora-timed means that each mora tends to take about the same amount of time to pronounce. English being stress-timed means that, as you can verify by tapping on the stressed syllables of example (6), the time that elapses between major stresses tends to be roughly constant.

mora-timed＝
モーラで調子を合わせる
mora＝拍，モーラ
stress-timed＝
強勢で調子を合わせる

(6) Strésses ténd to occúr at régular íntervals.

Yet another major difference between the two languages concerns syllable structure, the arrangement of consonants (C) and vowels (V) into syllables. In Japanese, most syllables are **open**— that is, they end in vowels. The exceptions are combinations of the form (C)＋V＋っ and (C)＋V＋ん, as in ほったん [hottan]. These sequences, then, constitute **closed** syllables, syllables that end in consonants (assuming, as suggested above, that the syllable is defined as the domain of accent). In English, closed syllables are more common and take a much greater variety of

open syllable＝開音節

closed syllable＝閉音節

forms. Contrast, for example, the English and Japanese words meaning 'chocolate'. English *chocolate* is pronounced [tʃáklət] and thus consists of two closed syllables. Japanese チョコレート is pronounced [tʃokoréeto] and thus consists of four open syllables.

VOWELS AND CONSONANTS CD Track 21

We have spent a large portion of this chapter talking about intonation, accent, and syllable structure because an awareness of the characteristics of English and the differences between English and Japanese in these areas is very helpful for the Japanese student of English. Asked to give representative examples of differences between the sound systems of English and Japanese, however, many people would probably think first of differences in the system of consonants and vowels. For example, English distinguishes [ɹ] and [l] while Japanese does not, and English distinguishes [æ] and [ʌ] (the vowels of *bat* and *but*, respectively) while Japanese does not. As a result of these two differences, English *ranch*, which begins with [ɹæ], and English *lunch*, which begins with [lʌ], are realized identically when borrowed into Japanese, namely as ランチ. In this last section of the chapter, we will survey English consonants and vowels. As you read the section below, please refer to Figure 1.

1. nasal cavity（鼻腔）
2. lips（唇）
3. teeth（歯）
4. alveolar ridge（歯茎隆起）
5. hard palate（硬口蓋）
6. velum, soft palate（軟口蓋）
7. uvula（口蓋垂，のどひこ）
8. tongue tip（舌尖）
9. tongue body（舌体）
10. vocal cords（声帯）
11. oral cavity（口腔）
12. glottis（声門）

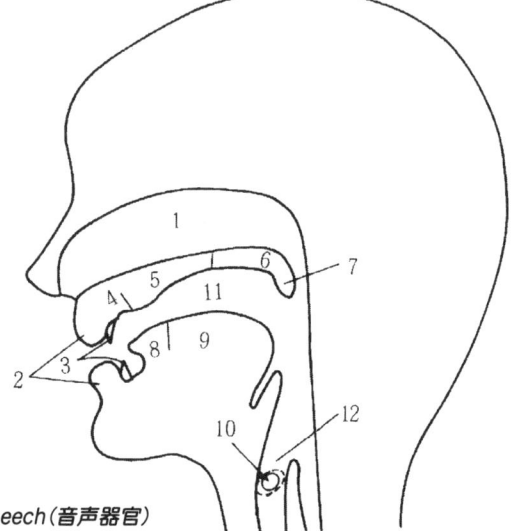

Figure 1 Organs of Speech（音声器官）

obstruct = 阻害する	

Consonants can be classified according to the degree to which the flow of air through the mouth is **obstructed** during their production. **Stops** like [p], [b], or [m] involve a total **obstruction** of the airflow in the mouth, and **fricatives** like [s] and [z] involve obstruction of the airflow to the point where it becomes rough and noisy. Stops and fricatives can be further classified according to whether they are **voiced** (accompanied by vocal cord vibration), like [d] and [z], or **voiceless**, like [t] and [s]. Stops may be further classified according to whether they are **nasal** (pronounced with the **soft palate** down so that air flows out through the nose as well as through the mouth), like [n], or **oral**, like [t] and [d]. Below, we will make use of **binary** (two-valued) **features** in classifying sounds. Among these will be [stop], where stops are [+stop] and all other sounds are [−stop]; [voice], where voiced sounds are [+voice] and voiceless sounds are [−voice]; and [nasal], where nasal sounds are [+nasal] and oral sounds are [−nasal].

Consonants can also be classified according to their **point of articulation**, or location (along a front-to-back line) at which the obstruction that characterizes the consonant is made. For English consonants, the relevant points of articulation are (1) **bilabial** (BL), referring to an obstruction made with the lower lip against the upper lip; (2) **labio-dental** (LD; lower lip against upper teeth); (3) **(inter)dental** (ID; tongue tip or blade against upper teeth, where the blade of the tongue is the flexible portion behind the tip); (4) **alveolar** (AL; tongue blade against **alveolar ridge**); (5) **palato-alveolar** (PA; tongue blade against the sloping region between the alveolar ridge and the **hard palate** proper); and (6) **velar** (VE; tongue body against soft palate (**velum**)). In Table 1 below we show all English stops and fricatives, classified by point of articulation and the three features [voice], [stop], and [nasal]. The only English consonants that do not appear in that table are the **semivowels** [j] and [w], the **liquids** [ɹ] and [l], and the **glottal fricative** [h].

Glossary (margin):

- obstruct = 阻害する
- stop = 閉鎖音
- obstruction = 阻害
- fricative = 摩擦音
- voiced = 有声
- vocal cord = 声帯
- voiceless = 無声
- nasal = 鼻音
- soft palate = 軟口蓋
- oral = 口音
- binary features = 二項素性
- point of articulation = 調音点
- bilabial = 両唇音
- labio-dental = 唇歯音
- (inter)dental = 歯間音
- tongue tip = 舌尖（せん）
- tongue blade = 舌端
- alveolar = 歯茎音
- alveolar ridge = 歯槽隆起
- palato-alveolar = 硬口蓋歯茎音
- hard palate = 硬口蓋
- velar = 軟口蓋音
- velum = 軟口蓋
- semivowel = 半母音
- liquid = 流音
- glottal fricative = 声門摩擦音

Chapter 9 The Sounds of English: Phonetics and Phonology

	BL	LD	ID	AL	PA	VE
[−voice, −stop, −nasal]		f	θ	s	ʃ	
[+voice, −stop, −nasal]		v	ð	z	ʒ	
[−voice, +stop, −nasal]	p			t	tʃ	k
[+voice, +stop, −nasal]	b			d	dʒ	g
[+voice, +stop, +nasal]	m			n		ŋ

Table 1 English stops and fricatives

Let us now consider the English vowel system. English vowels are subject to a good deal of dialectal variation; here we will describe the vowels of a variety of English spoken over much of the central and western area of the United States and much of Canada. While from one point of view the vowel system of this variety of English has twenty members, we will see that they can all be described in terms of six short vowels that may optionally be followed by [j], [w], or [ɹ]. To begin with, the six short vowels are those of Table 2. There they are represented by the appropriate symbol of the **IPA** (International Phonetic Alphabet) and by a one-syllable word. They are also classified according to the features [**high**], [**low**], and [**back**], which refer in principle to the position of the highest point of the tongue.

dialectal variation = 方言差

IPA = 国際音声字母

high = 高舌
low = 低舌
back = 後舌

	[−back]	[+back]
[+high]	[ɪ] pit	[ʊ] put
[−high, −low]	[ɛ] pet	[ʌ] putt
[+low]	[æ] pat	[ɑ] pot (also *caught*, etc.)

Table 2 English short vowels

Of the vowels of Table 2, those that are [−back] combine with [j] and those that are [+back] combine with [w], producing the six long vowels of Table 3:

	[−back]	[+back]
[+high]	[ij] beat	[uw] boot
[−high, −low]	[ej] bait	[ow] boat
[+low]	[aj] bite	[aw] bout

Table 3 English long vowels (Set I)

phonological＝音韻的

Note that most of the vowels of Table 1 change their values slightly in combination with [j] or [w]. We will consider this variation to be the result of general phonological rules. Perhaps the most obvious of these is the rule that changes [ʌ] to [o] before [w].

Finally, the variety of English we are describing has a set of six vowels that end in the element [ɹ]. One of these is [ɹː], as in *burr* [bɹː]; the other five have an initial element that, as with the long vowels of Table 3, can be identified with a short vowel from Table 2:

	[−back]	[+back]
[+high]	[iɹ] beer	[uɹ] boor
[−high, −low]	[ɛɹ] bear	[ɔɹ] bore
[+low]		[ɑɹ] bar

Table 4 English long vowels (Set II)

Apart from [ɹː], the only vowels not included in Tables 2-4 are [ɔj] (*boy*) and [juw] (*butte*), which can be identified with the combinations [ʌ] + [j] and [i] + [w], respectively. We thus see that while the English vowel system looks quite complicated, it can be constructed, with the help of a small number of phonological rules, from the six short vowels of Table 2 plus the elements [j], [w], and [ɹ].

Comprehension Check
✎ 空所を埋めなさい。

文全体の調子の上がり下がりを（　　　）という。断定を表す文では文末が（　　　）になり，疑問や疑いを表す文は文末が（　　　）になる。この音声的な違いは，平叙文と疑問文の統語構造（語順）より（　　　）。つまり，This is mine. のように構文的には平叙文であっても，文末が上昇イントネーションになると，意味は（　　　）になる。イントネーションが文全体に係わるのに対して，語や句の中で音声上際立った部分は（　　　）と呼ばれる。これには，英語の permít と pérmit に見られるような（　　　）と，日本語の「花」と「鼻」に見られるような（　　　）がある。「花」と「鼻」は，「は」と「な」の高低で区別されるだけで，調子が高くても

低くても,「あ」という母音そのものの音質は変わらない。ところが,英語のアクセントは強弱であるので,弱い母音は（　　　）になってしまう。そうすると,日本語のリズムは,「は」とか「な」といった（　　　）を単位にして均等に時間が割り振られるが,英語のほうは,（　　　）の置かれる位置がほぼ均等な間隔になる。

Exercises

(1) A さんと B さんの会話で, B さんのイントネーションを次のようにすると, どのようなニュアンスが伝えられるか説明しなさい。

1. A: Would you like something to drink ?
   B: Yes. Iced coffee.
2. A: Your boss said you're fired.
   B: Excuse me.
3. A: Do you know the answer ?
   B: Do YOU know the answer ?（YOU を強く）

(2) 各組で, 英語の音節数と日本語のモーラ数を比べなさい。

a. strike と「ストライキ」　　b. hamburger と「ハンバーガー」
c. rhythm と「リズム」　　　d. assistant と「アシスタント」

(3) 次の英文で, 強勢のある部分に鋭アクセント記号（´）を付け, stress-timed rhythm になるように, 声を出して発音しなさい。

a. I left my heart in San Francisco.（song title）
b. It rains, it hails, it batters, it blows, and I am wet through all my clothes.（from a nursery rhyme）

(4) 各組で示された単語を声を出して発音し, 左側と右側の発音がどのように違っているか説明しなさい。

a. pick と pig
b. sheet と seat
c. heat と feet
d. 英語 hit の出だしの音と, 日本語「ヒット」の出だしの音
e. 英語 park の終わりの音と, 日本語「パーク」の終わりの音

f. 英語 park の出だし音と，日本語「パーク」の出だしの音

g. 英語 work の真ん中の音と，日本語「ワーク」の真ん中の音

h. 英語 who の出だしの音と，日本語「ふ(負)」の出だしの音

(5) 次のカタカナ日本語に対応する英語を正しいつづりで示し，その発音を IPA 記号で書きなさい。

a. コットン(綿)　　　　　b. マクドナルド(人名)
c. ラップ(食品を包むフィルム)　d. ラップ(走路の一周)

(6) 次の素性の組み合わせが表す英語の短母音を IPA 記号で示しなさい。また，その母音を含む単語を挙げなさい(p.109 の Table2)。

a. [＋back, ＋high]　b. [－back, ＋high]　c. [－back, ＋low]

(7) 次の素性の組み合わせが表す英語の子音を IPA で示しなさい(p.109 の Table1)。

a. [＋voice, －stop, －nasal, ＋labio-dental]
b. [－voice, ＋stop, －nasal, ＋velar]
c. [＋nasal, ＋velar]

(8) 各組で 2 つの単語(ないし形態素)が 1 語にまとまったとき，別々の場合と比べて発音がどのように変わるか説明しなさい。

a. news と paper が複合されて newspaper になると。
b. cup と board が複合されて cupboard になると。
c. church と hill が複合されて Churchill(人名)になると。
d. 否定の接頭辞 in- が possible について impossible になると。
e. 否定の接頭辞 in- が regular について irregular になると。

長い母音の発音

　本章ではアメリカ中西部とカナダの大部分で話されている英語の母音について学んだ。本文にもあるように，母音の発音には顕著な地域差が観察される。

　以下はオーストラリアの病院での患者と看護士の会話である。アメリカ人の患者が意識を失ったまま病院に担ぎ込まれた。気づいてみると，病院のベッドの上。ずっと眠っていたようだが，一体どのぐらい時間がたったのだろうと思って，"Did I come here yesterday?" と尋ねると，"No, you came here today." 患者はがっくり…オーストラリア英語では [ej] が [aj] と発音されるため，患者は看護士の答えを "No, you came here to die." と解釈したという笑い話である ([tədéj] "today" [tədáj]= "to die")。

　以前はオーストラリア英語特有とされていたこの発音は，近年イギリス人の間でもかなり広がってきている。例えば，サッカーのベッカムとその夫人の英語にも，この傾向がはっきりあらわれ，painting が「ペインティング」ではなく「パインティン」のように聞こえる。

　次章ではこのような英語の地域差を取り上げる。

Chapter 10 Regional Varieties of English: Sociolinguistics I

BASIC QUESTIONS
英語は，世界のさまざまな国でコミュニケーションの手段として，広範に使用されている。地域によって，どのような違いがあるのだろうか。英語にも，日本語と同じように，標準語と方言があるのだろうか。

ENGLISHES IN THE WORLD

According to David Crystal's *The Cambridge Encyclopedia of the English Language* (1995), English is spoken as a **native language** by some 377 million people around the world. It is used as the exclusive language of the majority of speakers in Great Britain, the United States, Canada, Australia, and New Zealand. English has also become the predominant **second language** in such areas as India, Pakistan, Bangladesh, Singapore, Hong Kong, the Philippines, and substantial parts of Africa, where it coexists with other languages. English is a truly international language. However, the way in which English is spoken and written varies from place to place.

native language = 母語

second language = 第二言語

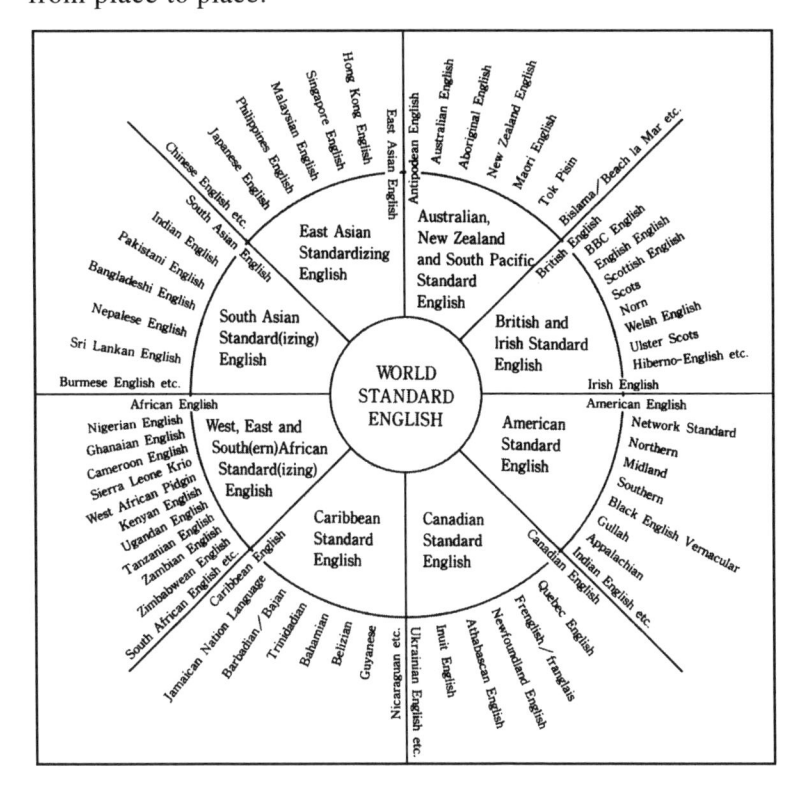

Figure 1 World Englishes
(T. McArthur "The English Languages?" *English Today* 1987)

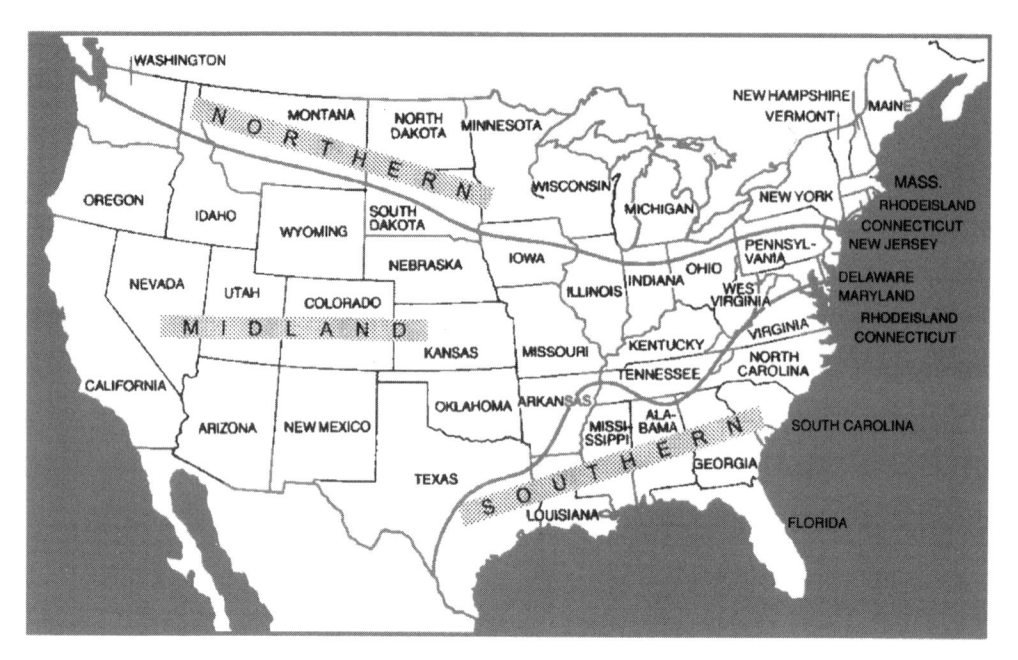

Map 1 Dialect areas of the mainland U.S.
(D. Crystal *The English Language* 1988: 225)

REGIONAL DIALECTS

Versions of a language used by only some of its speakers are often referred to as **varieties** of that language. The term **regional dialect** refers to those distinguished from each other in terms of geography. As you have probably experienced when traveling, the way people speak varies from place to place, and the differences may be great enough to result in miscommunication.

Regional dialects differ in pronunciation, grammar, vocabulary, and spelling. The branch of linguistics that studies **regional variation** is called **dialectology**. The work of **dialectologists** usually takes the form of a **linguistic atlas** consisting of maps on which lexical, phonological, and syntactic differences are displayed. In this chapter, we will see that English displays a considerable degree of geographical variation intranationally (within a single country) as well as internationally.

variety =（言語）変種
regional dialect =
地理方言

regional variation =
地理的変異
dialectology = 方言学
dialectologist =
方言研究者
linguistic atlas =
言語地図

Chapter 10 Regional Varieties of English: Sociolinguistics I

Map 2 Dialect areas of England
(D. Crystal *The Cambridge Encyclopedia of the English Language.* Cambridge University Press 1995: 325)

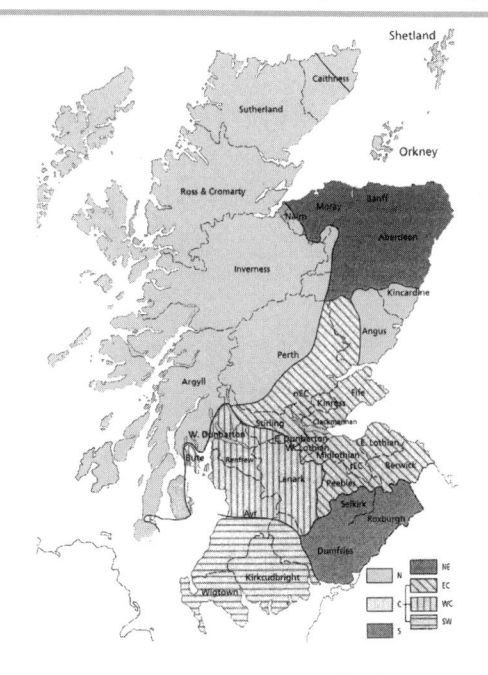

Map 3 Dialect areas of Scotland
(D. Crystal *The Cambridge Encyclopedia of the English Language.* Cambridge University Press 1995: 332)

INTRANATIONAL VARIATION

intranational＝国内部の

All over the world, dialectologists have identified features that distinguish groups of speakers from one another. First let us consider dialect differences within the United States. Speakers from the South **raise the vowel** [ɛ] to [ɪ] before nasals, causing *pin* and *pen*, *him* and *hem*, and *tin* and *ten* to **merge** into the same pronunciation.

raise the vowel＝母音の舌の位置を上げる
merge＝合一する

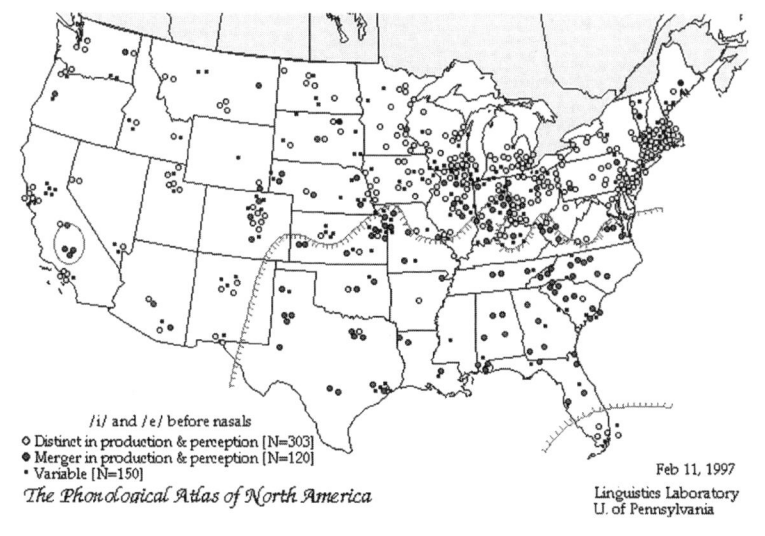

Map 4 The merger of [ɪ] and [ɛ] before nasals
http://www.ling.upenn.edu/phono_atlas/maps/Map3.html

homophonous＝同音の

accent＝
発音上の特徴(なまり)

Map 4 indicates that these words are **homophonous** in an area that is centered on the old South but extends westward into New Mexico and as far north as northern Kansas and Missouri. Regional dialects based on such phonological features are often called **accents**.

There are vocabulary differences among intranational varieties of English as well. *Dragonfly, darning needle, mosquito hawk, spindle, snake feeder, snake doctor,* and *snake waiter* all refer to the same kind of insect(トンボ); their geographical distribution in part of the Eastern United States can be seen in Map 5.

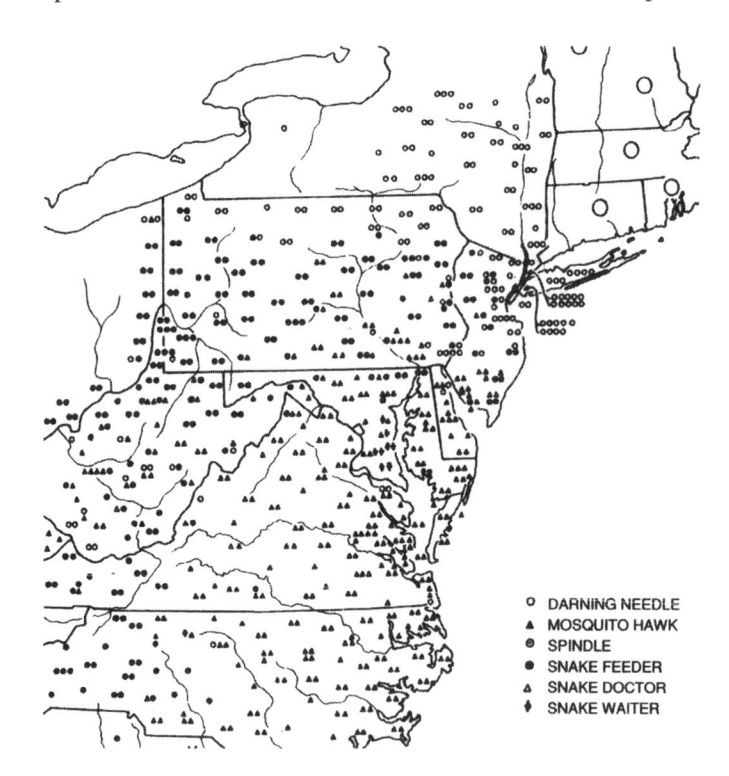

Map 5 Dialect map of 'dragonfly'
(H. Kurath *A Word Geography of the Eastern United States* 1949)

While dialectologists were originally interested almost exclusively in phonological and lexical differences, their interests have expanded in recent years to include syntactic or grammatical variation. As an illustration of grammatical variation in English, we show in Table 1 some traditional forms of the present tense of the verb *be* used in several regions of Great Britain. Compare

Standard	Kent	Yorkshire
I am we are	I are we are	I is we are
you are you are	you are you are	you is you are
(s)he is they are	(s)he is they are	(s)he is they are
Northumberland	**Somerset**	**Sussex**
I is we are	I be we be	I be we be
you are you are	you be you be	you be you be
(s)he is they are	(s)he is they be	(s)he be they be

Table 1 Varieties of *be*-verbs

them with the **standard forms** you learned at school. You will immediately notice that Standard English distinctions in person (first/second/third) and number (singular/plural) have been reduced or eliminated in the nonstandard dialects. For instance, in Yorkshire only the number distinction is retained (singular *is* vs. plural *are*), while in Sussex *be* is used throughout the paradigm (**invariant** *be*). In no nonstandard dialect does the first person singular show a distinctive form like standard *am*.

Map 6 English counties

INTERNATIONAL VARIATION

American English and **British English** are two major varieties of English. Let us first examine how they differ in spelling, or **orthography**. In Table 2, you will find a few common examples.

	American English	British English
-or/-our	honor, favor	honour, favour
-er/-re	meter, center	metre, centre
-ize/-ise	apologize, civilize	apologise, civilise
-dgment/-dgement	judgment	judgement
-led/-lled	canceled, channeled	cancelled, channelled

Table 2 Orthographic differences between American and British English

standard form＝標準語形
invariant *be*＝不変の be
American English＝
アメリカ英語
British English＝
イギリス英語
orthography＝
正書法（正しい綴り字）

There are also vocabulary differences. A Londoner takes a *lift*, but a New Yorker takes an *elevator*. In Table 3, you will find more examples of such lexical differences.

American English	British English
bathroom	toilet
apartment	flat
mouse pad	mouse mat
gas	petrol
line	queue
truck	lorry
a week from today	today week

Table 3 Lexical differences between American and British English

American English and British English differ from each other grammatically too. In Table 4, you will find some examples.

American English	British English
Do you have a pen?	Have you (got) a pen?
I've gotten used to the system.	I've got used to the system.

Table 4 Grammatical differences between American and British English

It should be noted, however, that in recent years, some of those orthographic, lexical, and grammatical differences have tended to be eliminated in favor of the American variant. One example is the *-ise/-ize* distinction, which used to be a hallmark of the difference between British and American English. Current dictionaries published in England do not list verb forms with *-ise* or noun forms with *-isation*, but show only the forms with *-ize* and *-ization*. A glance at a corpus of British English confirms that the frequencies of *realization* and *realisation* or *civilization* and *civilisation* in actual usage are almost fifty-fifty.

Let us now take a look at Canadian English. Although Canadian English is often regarded as a subvariety of North American English, it is distinct from American English in several ways. For example, a long upholstered seat that holds three or four people is called a *couch* in American English. Canadians, by contrast, call it a *chesterfield*. Terms such as *premier*(州の首相), *ridings*(選挙

upholstered＝
クッション付きの

区), and *reserve*(先住民住居区) are also uniquely Canadian. These lexical differences, too, however, have been disappearing. According to a recent survey, *chesterfield* has been losing ground to *couch* since the 1950s.

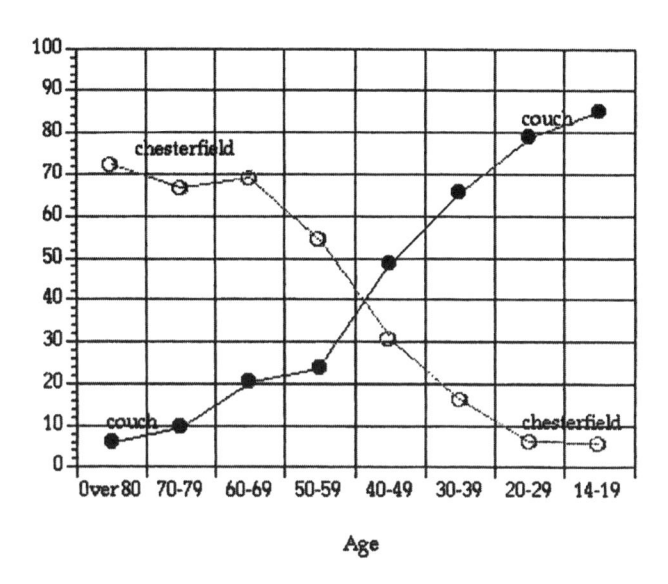

Figure 2 chesterfield *vs.* couch *in Canadian English*
(Conference Handbook 19, 2001 English Linguistic Society of Japan p.121)

International varieties typically show phonological differences as well. In England, Australia, New Zealand, South Africa and the West Indies (except Barbados), for example, people generally drop their *r*'s after a vowel (**post-vocalic *r***), as in [kɑː] *car* and [kɑːd] *card*. In Scotland, Ireland, most of North America and Barbados, on the other hand, people retain these *r*'s, pronouncing these words as [kɑɹ] and [kɑɹd]. The former are **r-less** or **non-rhotic** speakers whereas the latter are **r-full**, or **rhotic** speakers. For this variable we also find regional differences within a single country. Maps 7 and 8 show that post-vocalic *r* is retained in some areas of England but lost in eastern New England, metropolitan New York, and the coastal plain of the South in the United States. Whether post-vocalic *r* is pronounced or not is considered to be one of the most distinctive features of an English dialect.

post-vocalic *r* =
母音の後の r

r-less, non-rhotic =
母音の後の r を発音しない
r-full, rhotic =
母音の後の r を発音する

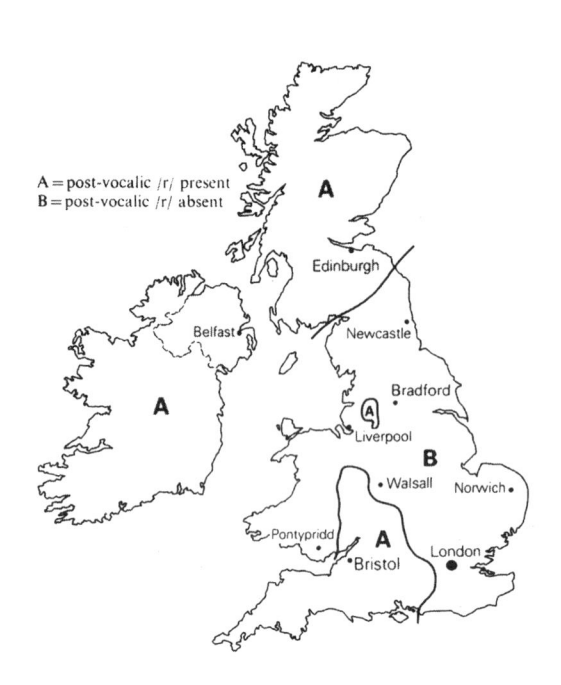

Map 7 Post vocalic r in England and Ireland
(A. Hughes and P. Trudgill
English Accents and Dialects.
Edward Arnold 1979: 33)

Map 8 Post vocalic r
in the Eastern United States
(W. Downes *Language and Society* 2nd ed.
Cambridge University Press 1998: 151)

Non-rhotic speakers retain a word final *r* when the first sound of the next word is a vowel. Thus we have:

[bɹʌðə]   brother

but

[bɹʌðəɹ ən sɪstə]   brother and sister

linking *r* = 連結の r

The *r* in the pronunciation of *brother and sister* is called **linking r**. Many non-rhotic speakers also insert an *r* where there is no *r* in the spelling as in:

the idea [ɹ] of it   draw[ɹ]ing

intrusive *r* = 嵌入の r
prescriptive = 規範的な

This phenomenon is known as **intrusive r**. Although intrusive *r* is considered "incorrect" by **prescriptive** grammarians, it is observed even in prestige non-rhotic dialects.

In this chapter, we have focused on regional varieties of English. We will find out more about the diversity of English in Chapter 11.

Comprehension Check

✏️ 空所を埋めなさい。

　英語をコミュニケーションの手段として日常的に使っている人々の数は非常に多い。このうち，イギリスやアメリカの人々は英語を（　　　）として，インドやシンガポールの人々は（　　　）として使用している。

　世界各地の英語は，地域によって（　　　），（　　　），（　　　），（　　　）が異なる。言語の地理的変種を（　　　）と呼び，それを研究する分野は（　　　）である。このような地理的変異は国家間にも，一国内の地方間にも存在する。アメリカ英語とイギリス英語にはさまざまなレベルで違いがあるが，現在は（　　　）式が優勢になりつつある。

Exercises

(1) 以下の各組はアメリカ英語とイギリス英語の綴りの違いを示している。（　　　）内に適切な綴りを入れなさい。また，右端に「類例」という欄がある場合は，その行と同じタイプの例を別に示しなさい。

アメリカ英語	イギリス英語	類例
connection	（　　　）	_____ / _____
harbor	（　　　）	_____ / _____
（　　　）	enquire	_____ / _____
（　　　）	acknowledgement	_____ / _____
catalog	（　　　）	_____ / _____
skillful	（　　　）	_____ / _____
program	（　　　）	_____ / _____
offense	（　　　）	_____ / _____
canceling	（　　　）	_____ / _____
（　　　）	woollen	
（　　　）	cheque（小切手）	
（　　　）	aluminium	［注：英米で発音も異なる］
airplane	（　　　）	［注：英米で発音も異なる］
jail	（　　　）	
（　　　）	three-storeyed	

(2) 同じ物を指すのに，イギリス英語とアメリカ英語では異なった単語が用いられることがある。空所に適切な語句を入れなさい。

アメリカ英語	イギリス英語	アメリカ英語	イギリス英語
subway	(　　　　)	zip code	(　　　　)
can opener	(　　　　)	(　　　　)	tap［水道の蛇口］
(　　　　)	waistcoat	potato chips	(　　　　)
(　　　　)	sweets	(　　　　)	pram
(　　　　)	biscuits	(　　　　)	Sellotape
(　　　　)	rubber［消しゴム］	(　　　　)	noticeboard

(3) either, schedule, tomato をそれぞれ，アメリカ英語とイギリス英語の発音で読んでみなさい。また，アメリカとイギリスで発音の違う単語を他に挙げなさい。

(4) インターネットで例を集めてみよう。

　　(1)～(3)の設問では「イギリス英語」と「アメリカ英語」の違いを見たが，実際のところ，イギリス／アメリカの区別は大雑把な目安にすぎず，イギリスの中にもアメリカ英語が入っているし，アメリカの中にもイギリス英語が入っている。このことをインターネットの Collins COBUILD Wordbanks（本書 p.90 参照）を活用して確かめてみよう。http://titania.cobuild.collins.co.uk/form.html を開くと，次のような欄が出てくる。

　　☐　British books, ephemera, radio, newspapers, magazines（26 m words）
　　☐　American books, ephemera and radio（9 m words）
　　☐　British transcribed speech（10 m words）

　1 番上にチェックを付けるとイギリスでの出版物，2 番目にチェックを付けるとアメリカでの出版物が検索の資料として選ばれる。例えば，autumn（秋）は一般にはイギリス英語と言われるが，アメリカで使われないのだろうか。"American books" のところだけにチェックを付けて，検索ウインドウに in+autumn と入力し，検索してみよう。それと比べて，"British books" だけをチェックして，同じ検索を行った場合はどのような結果になるだろうか。
　同じような比較を，語彙や綴りについて，できるだけたくさん試してみなさい。

ニューヨークかヌーヨークか？

　ネイティヴスピーカーの発音を聞いていると，new を「ニュー」ではなく「ヌー」と発音する人が案外多い。tune を「チューン」ではなく「トゥーン」と言うのも同じ種類の音声変化である。このように，子音の後に来る [juw] から [j] が取れて，[uw] と発音される現象は，j-dropping または yod-dropping と呼ばれ，アメリカおよびイギリスの両方で見られる。類例をあげてみよう。

　　dune[djuwn]〜[duwn], sue [sjuw]〜[suw], resume [ɹɪzjuwm]〜[ɹɪzuwm],
　　enthusiasm [ɛnθjuwziæzm]〜[ɛnθuwziæzm], lute [ljuwt]〜[luwt], rude [ɹuwd]

この現象は，[t d n s z θ l ɹ]，つまり歯間音および歯茎音の後で起こる。したがって pure, beauty, music, future, view, cute, hue などの語では観察されない（ただし，イギリスの East Anglia は yod-dropping が最も進んでいる地域で，すべての語で起こる）。下表は，イギリス英語とアメリカ英語で，この現象が生起する音声環境をまとめたものである。yes は常に，variable は場合によっては yod-dropping が起こることを表す。no の環境では起こらない。

	British English	American English
t_	no	variable
d_	no	variable
n_	no	variable
s_	variable	yes
z_	variable	yes
θ_	variable	yes
l_	variable	yes
ɹ_	yes	yes

アメリカ英語でもイギリス英語でも，[ɹ] の後には [j] がない。アメリカ英語では，その他に [s z θ l] の後でも yod-dropping が観察されるが，閉鎖音である [t d n] の後ではいつも生起するわけではない。これに対して，イギリス英語では，[j] が常にないのは [ɹ] の後のみである。yod-dropping は [s z θ l] の後では時々起こり，閉鎖音 [t d n] の後では起こらない。全体的に見ると，この現象はアメリカ英語に一般的である（注：アメリカの中でも，西へ行けば行くほど，[j] 抜きの発音をする話者が多くなる）。

Chapter 11　English in Society: Sociolinguistics II

> **BASIC QUESTIONS**
> 電話で少し話しただけで，一度も会ったことのない相手の出身地だけでなく，社会的背景についても，ある程度見当がつくのはどうしてだろうか。

SOCIAL VARIATION　Track 22

In the previous chapter, the focus was on regional variation in English. In this chapter we turn our attention to **social variation** within a single **speech community**.

Every professional and occupational group has **jargon**—that is, language that is obscure or unintelligible to outsiders. An example is the technical terms of linguistics contained in this book, such as *morpheme, polysemy,* and *dialect,* which are not well understood by non-linguists. Likewise, students and faculty members of a particular university tend to use words and expressions whose meaning is clear only to those who belong to that group. The Japanese word フラ語, shortened from フランス語, for example, will be understood only by university students. You can probably think of similar examples like パン教（＜一般教養），援部（＜応援指導部），クラ友（＜クラスの友達），and ビー部（＜ラグビー部）. These examples illustrate how language signals group membership.

The way someone talks often reveals not only his or her regional origin but also, in many cases, his or her social background, including factors such as occupation and educational level. How people speak is strongly correlated with their membership in various groups. Those who belong to the same social group tend to speak in a similar way. These social speech varieties are called **social dialects** or **sociolects**.

social variation = 社会的変異
speech community = 言語共同体
jargon = 隠語
technical terms = 専門用語

social dialect, sociolect = 社会方言

STANDARD VS. NONSTANDARD ENGLISH　Track 23

In a modern society, there is usually one sociolect or variety of a language that is dominant with respect to the others. The term

standard=標準

non-standard=非標準

standard refers to this dominant or prestige variety. This is the variety that is used by the mass media and taught in schools. Other varieties are **non-standard**.

GRAMMATICAL VARIATION CD Track 24

In Chapter 10, we examined standard and non-standard forms of the present tense of the verb *be*. What about the forms of other verbs? In standard English, verbs in the present tense with third person singular subjects have an inflectional ending written -*(e)s*. In many non-standard varieties, this suffix also occurs with subjects representing other person-number combinations. Examples like (1)-(3), taken from recorded conversations in *The British National Corpus,* are by no means rare in non-standard English.

(1) I want<u>s</u> some more bread.
(2) Now you know<u>s</u> why he stays quiet.
(3) Is that how fast they go<u>es</u>?

African American Vernacular English=
アフリカ系アメリカ人日常英語

In some dialects, on the other hand, third person singular -*s* is absent. Figure 1 illustrates the patterning of this phenomenon in **African American Vernacular English**(**AAVE**), a non-standard variety that was formerly called "Black English" and has been investigated extensively. Each bar indicates the percentage of *s*-less forms in the speech of the corresponding socioeconomic class. You can see a striking difference between the **middle-class** groups(UM, LM) and the **working-class** groups(UW, LW).

middle-class=中流階級
working-class=労働者階級

UM(upper middle)=
上層中流
LM(lower middle)=
下層中流
UW(upper working)=
上層労働者
LW(lower working)=
下層労働者

	UM	LM	UW	LW
Mean percent -s absence	1.4	9.7	56.9	71.4

UM = upper middle class; LM = lower middle class; UW = upper working class; LW = lower working class.

Figure 1 Absence of third person singular -s
(Wolfram and Schilling-Estes(1998) *American English,* p. 156)

Let us now turn to the past tense forms of verbs. We will review the forms of standard English first. The past tense forms of **regular verbs** are made by adding an ending written *-ed* and pronounced as indicated in (4).

regular verb=規則動詞

(4) Regular past tense *-ed* in standard English
 a. [əd]: (after *t* and *d*): painted, wanted, molded, handed
 b. [t]: (otherwise after [−voice] sounds): coughed, missed, talked, jumped
 c. [d]: (otherwise): lived, rubbed, remained, sighed

The great majority of English verbs belong to this group. However, there are a significant number of **irregular verbs** as well. The past tense forms of irregular verbs are formed in one of the following ways.

irregular verb=不規則動詞

(5) Irregular past tense forms in standard English
 a. no change: *hit-hit, cut-cut*
 b. change of final [d] to [t]: *send-sent*
 c. vowel change: *give-gave, light-lit, sing-sang, fly-flew*
 d. vowel change and suffixation: *feel-felt, tell-told*
 e. vowel change, deletion of final consonant, and suffixation: *bring-brought*

Contrary to what the names "regular" and "irregular" suggest, irregular verbs like the ones just illustrated are actually used much more frequently than regular verbs, and they tend to resist change. In non-standard English, however, past tense forms of irregular verbs are often different from the standard English forms. Here are some examples.

(6) a. regular suffixation instead of vowel change

present tense	nonstandard past	standard past
blow	blowed	blew
hold	holded	held
give	gived	gave
run	runned	ran
fight	fighted	fought

 b. present tense form used as past tense form

present tense	nonstandard past	standard past
take	take	took
forget	forget	forgot
run	run	ran
break	break	broke
throw	throw	threw

past participle=過去分詞

c. new irregular past form derived under the influence of other irregular verbs or of the **past participle** form

present tense	nonstandard past	standard past
write	writ	wrote
drive	driv	drove
ride	rid	rode
bring	brang	brought

Here are some actual examples taken from *The British National Corpus*.

(7) I <u>blowed</u> my nose.
(8) I expect he <u>gived</u> you a funny answer.
(9) He <u>writ</u> and told them he'd finished; then we all finished.

We may observe that past tense forms in non-standard varieties tend to be more uniformly marked with the regular *-ed* inflection than those in standard English. Regularization of irregular verbs in non-standard dialects represents the continuation of a process that has operated throughout the recorded history of English: historically speaking, many English verbs that are regular today belonged to the irregular group in Old English and have changed over the centuries to conform to the regular *-ed* pattern. Regularization of this sort is sometimes said to proceed by **analogy** with already existing patterns.

analogy=類推

double negation=二重否定

The use of **double negation**, as in *They don't know nothing*, is another typical feature of several English sociolects. Look at the following examples.

affirmative=肯定

(10)	standard English	non-standard English
affirmative	1a. They know something.	2a. They know something.
negative	1b. They don't know anything.	2b. They don't know nothing.
	1c. They know nothing.	2c. They know nothing.

indefinite pronoun=不定代名詞

prescriptive grammar=規範文法

In standard English, when the verb is negated, the **indefinite pronoun** *something* becomes *anything* (1b). In non-standard English, on the other hand, it becomes *nothing* (2b). Some people, particularly those who have been influenced by prescriptive or school grammar, will claim that the two negative elements of (2b) (*-n't* and *nothing*) cancel each other out, and thus that

that sentence is either affirmative or illogical. Most native speakers of English, however, even those who don't use forms like (2b), know that (1b) and (2b) mean the same thing. Double negation was quite common in earlier English historically, as it is today in numerous varieties.

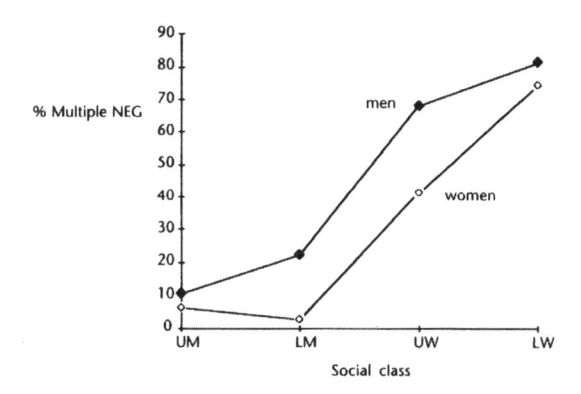

Figure 2 Percentage of multiple negation by women and men in Detroit (Wolfram 1969: 162, cited in J. K. Chambers(2003) *Sociolinguistic Theory*, p.131)

Figure 2 represents the patterning of double negation in Detroit. It shows a striking picture of social class difference again. Double negation is much more common among working-class speakers. Figure 2 presents **gender differentiation** as well. We will discuss how language and gender interact later in this chapter.

gender differentiation=
性差

Although you may have been surprised by the discrepancies between what you were taught in high-school English class and what you have seen above, "incorrect" verb forms like the ones illustrated are common in non-standard varieties of English, and may even show up from time to time in the speech of speakers of standard varieties. Further, such forms are "incorrect" only from a prescriptive point of view. Since the goal of linguistics is not to prescribe correct usage, but to account for the knowledge that every human being has concerning his or her native language, linguists do not judge any form to be correct or incorrect. Linguistically speaking, all varieties of a language are created equal.

prescribe=
こうあるべきだと定める

PHONOLOGICAL VARIATION 　CD Track 25

Cockney =
コクニー（ロンドン，イーストエンドの労働者のことば）
Eliza Doolittle =
イライザ・ドゥーリトル
Bernard Shaw =
バーナード・ショー

The **Cockney** dialect spoken by working class residents of the City of London is a typical example of a non-standard dialect. Eliza Doolittle, a character in Bernard Shaw's play *Pygmalion*, is a speaker of this sociolect. Her pronunciation is quite different from standard British English as you can see from the transcription below (and as you can hear in the film version of the play, *My Fair Lady,* starring Audrey Hepburn). We give Eliza's speech first in Shaw's spelling and then in standard English orthography.

(11) Cockney
Ow, eez, yə ooa san, is e? Wal, fewd dan y' d-ooty bawɪnz a mather should, eed now bettern to spawl a pore geɫ's flahrzn than ran awy athaht pyin. Will ye-oo py me f'them?

Standard Orthography
Oh, <u>h</u>e's your son, is <u>h</u>e? Well, if you'd done your duty by <u>h</u>im as a mother should, <u>h</u>e'd know better than to spoil a poor girl's flowers and then run away without payin[g]. Will you pay me for them?

In Cockney, the initial [h] (underlined above) in words like *he* and *him* is almost always absent. This sociolect also has the following features.

glottal stop = 声門閉鎖音（「アッ」の「ッ」のように，のどで息を止めた音）
environment =
（言語的な）環境

- The **glottal stop** [ʔ] as a replacement of [t] is extremely common between vowels and before a pause as in *butter* and *wet*.
- In most linguistic environments, [θ] and [ð] become [f] and [v], respectively.
    word-initially 　<u>th</u>in [f]
    word-medially 　Ca<u>th</u>y [f]　bro<u>th</u>er [v]
    word-finally 　ba<u>th</u> [f]　ba<u>th</u>e [v]

affricate = 破擦音

- Word initial [t] becomes an **affricate** [ts], as in *tea* [tsiː]

linguistic variable =
言語変項

You may also have noticed that *-ing* is pronounced [in] in Cockney (*pyin* vs. *payin*[g]). *-ing* is a **linguistic variable** not only in the Cockney dialect but also in English speech communities around the world. Its pronunciation varies not only among speakers (**interspeaker variation**) but often within the speech of a single individual (**intraspeaker variation**). For instance, *running* may be pronounced [ɹʌnɪŋ] or [ɹʌnɪn] either by different individuals or by the same individual at different times. Research has repeat-

interspeaker variation =
個人間変異
intraspeaker variation =
個人内変異

edly shown that diverse regional dialects are remarkably consistent with respect to the patterns of social variation for this variable. Speakers of higher social status and with higher education tend to use [ɪŋ] more frequently, and so do women.

No one speaks exactly the same all the time. Everybody, for example, is able to move back and forth between **formal** and **informal styles**. *-ing* tends to be pronounced as [ɪŋ] in formal situations, when speakers pay careful attention to their speech.

Figures 3 and 4 show the percentage of [in] in Norwich, England, and in New York City. The Norwich speakers are divided into five social groups, and New York speakers into four. The different styles in which their speech was recorded are shown from the most formal (reading aloud) to the most informal (free conversation). We can see from both figures that speakers use the standard pronunciation ([ɪŋ]) more often in the more careful styles, and that speakers in the higher social classes use [ɪŋ] more often in any given style.

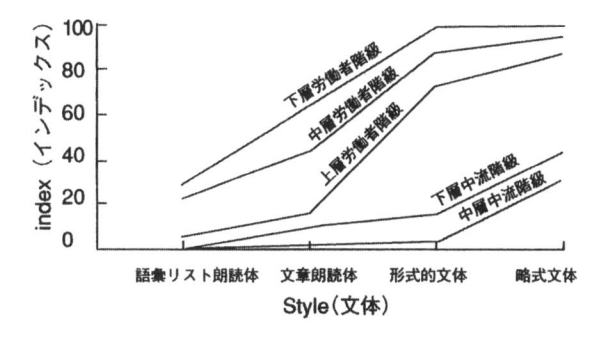

Figure 3 (P. Trudgill *The Social Differentiation of English in Norwich* 1974: 92)
（中尾・日比谷・服部『社会言語学概論』(1997) より引用 p.49）

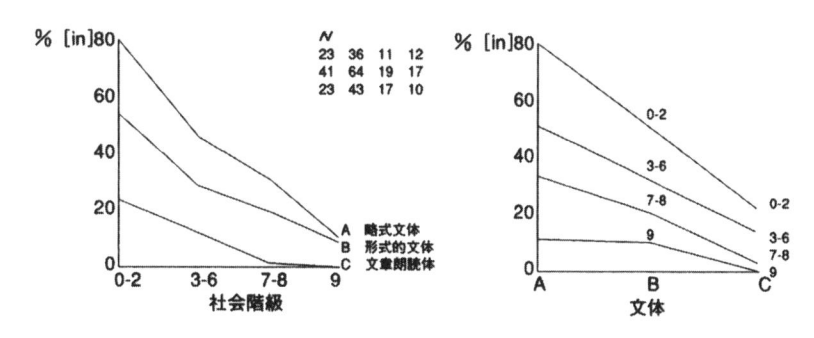

Figure 4 (W. Labov *The Social Stratification of English in New York City* 1966: 274)
（中尾・日比谷・服部『社会言語学概論』(1997) より引用 p.50）

LEXICAL VARIATION **CD** Track 26

Speakers of Standard British English (SBE) and Cockney also use different vocabulary items, as the following example illustrates:

(12) **SBE**: What an absolutely delightful meal this lunch was, thank you.
Cockney: Wha' an absolu'ee deligh'fuw meaw vis dinner was, cheers ma'e.

At midday, the SBE speaker has lunch while the Cockney speaker eats dinner. After the meal, the former says "thank you" to his or her host while the latter says "cheers ma'e (= mate)."

LANGUAGE AND GENDER **CD** Track 27

Men and women speak differently from each other in probably every speech community. Japan is a good example of this generalization, although **gender differences** in Japanese are less pronounced than they used to be as the result of the social changes the country has undergone since the Meiji period.

gender difference＝性差

Four decades of empirical research carried out in a wide variety of speech communities has repeatedly shown that women tend to use more standard forms than men do. In Figure 2 above, we saw one such instance. Let us consider some more examples. In virtually all studies conducted in English-speaking communities, there is evidence that women use more [-ɪŋ] and fewer [-ɪn] pronunciations than men in words like *speaking* and *reading*. As we have seen, in Cockney, [θ] often becomes [f]. In the African American Vernacular English spoken in Detroit, that consonant is realized as [θ], [f], [t] or ∅ (dropped) in non-initial position. The standard pronunciation is [θ]. In Figure 5, we see that women consistently use more standard forms in every social class except the lower working class.

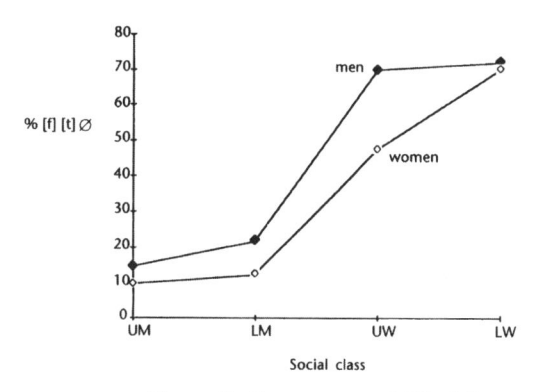

*Figure 5 Percentage of [f], [t],
and 0 variants as opposed to standard [θ]*
(Wolfram 1969: 92, cited in J. K. Chambers *Sociolinguistic Theory* 2003, p.128)

In earlier studies, gender was regarded as something static that men and women were born with. Speakers were categorized depending on their biological **sex**. In a pioneer study, Robin Lakoff pointed out the characteristic features of women's language, including the following:

sex＝生物学的な性

(13) a. Women tend to use rising intonation in declarative sentences more frequently than men.
   b. Women tend to use **tag questions** more often than men. (*This is nice, isn't it?*)
   c. Women tend to use **hedges** like *kind of* and *you know* more often than men.
   d. Women tend to use the emphatic *so* (called **feminine** *so*) more often than men. (*He is so kind.*)

tag question＝付加疑問

hedge＝ぼかしことば

feminine *so* ＝
女性語の so

Many detailed studies, however, have since shown that the relation between language and gender is not so simple. In recent studies, a more dynamic and elaborate approach has been proposed. In this view, gender is regarded as something men and women "perform" in a given social setting. Let us discuss a concrete example.

gender＝社会的な性

It is well-documented that Japanese **postpositional particles** are dropped in casual speech, as in (14).

postpositional particle＝
（名詞のあとにつける）助詞

(14) *watashi-wa   gohan-o   taberu.*
     watashi- 0   gohan- 0   taberu.

Varbrul Weight = weights or values associated with each factor independetly of the other factors. Larger weights indicate stronger effects.

S-S-D = same-sex dyadic conversations (2 males or 2 females)

M-S-D = cross-sex dyadic conversations (1 male + 1 female)

H-G = heterosexual group conversation (4 males and 3 females)

ellipsis = 省略

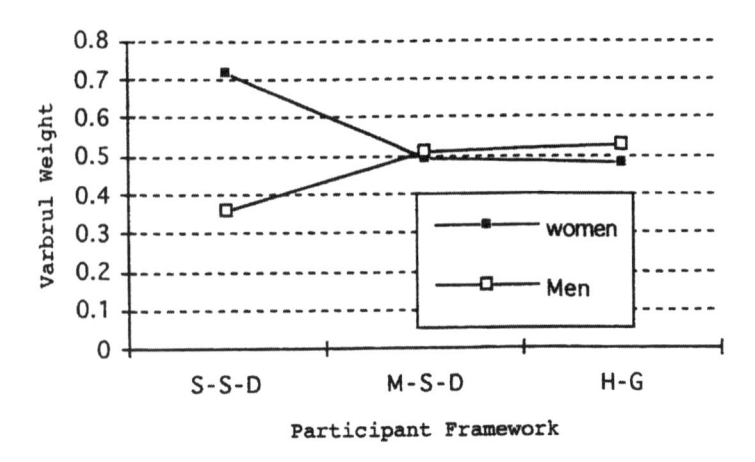

Figure 6 (S.Takano *"A quantitative study of gender differences in the ellipsis of the Japanese postpositional particles -wa and -ga: Gender composition as a constraint on variability,* 1998: 308)

Figure 6 clearly indicates that the rate of **ellipsis** varies from one type of conversational setting to another. Women drop particles much more often than men when they are engaged in conversations with another woman (S-S-D), whereas particle ellipsis occurs at virtually the same rate as men in cross-gender group interactions. These results suggest that the categorical treatment of gender (male or female) is inadequate to account for its relation to language. Both men and women are sensitive to the gender composition of conversational groups.

In this chapter, we have seen how our group affiliations are signaled by the speech forms we use. Social class, gender, age, and ethnicity are important dimensions of individual identity in many speech communities.

Comprehension Check

✎ 空所を埋めなさい。

英語の変種は，地域によって異なるだけではない。同一の（　　　）の内部でも人によって発音・文法・使用語彙が異なることがある。通常，社会的に同じグループに属する人々の使用する言語には何らかの共通性がある。このようなバリエーションは（　　　）と呼ばれ，各グループの使う言語を（　　　）という。グループ化は（　　　），（　　　），（　　　）などを基準にして行われる。

同一の地域に住んでいる，同一の社会的グループに所属する人々の間でも，使用する言語は常に同じというわけではない。われわれは言語の使用場面に応じて，発音や語形を変えており，（　　　）スタイルで話す時と（　　　）スタイルで話す時のことばは決して同じではない。

ロンドンの（　　　）や，米国全体に話者が広がっている（　　　）系アメリカ人日常英語は，典型的な（　　　）である。

言語の男女差は，早くから研究されていたが，最近は性を（　　　）にではなく（　　　）にとらえて分析するようになっている。

Exercises

(1) あなたの大学ではよく使われるが，外部の人には何のことだか分からない語や表現を5つ列挙し，それぞれが何を指すか，どのようにして形成されたかを説明しなさい。

(2) いわゆる「業界用語」を集めなさい（たとえば，アルバイト先で使われている用語，クラブ活動関係の用語，芸能人の用語など）。

(3) Lexical Variation の節で示したコクニーの例(12)には，本文の説明では触れなかった発音上の特徴が1つ含まれている。それは何か説明しなさい。

　　SBE: What an absolutely delightful meal this lunch was, thank you.
　　Cockney: Wha' an absolu'ee deligh'fuw meaw vis dinner was, cheers ma'e.

(4) [θ] と [ð] は本文で触れたように，コクニーでは [f] と [v] と発音されるが，他の多くの英語変種では [t] と [d] と発音されることも多い。下図はニューヨーク英語とフィラデルフィア英語で [ð] が [d] と発音される頻度を，話者の社会階層別・文体別に示したものである。この図からどんなことが分かるか，説明しなさい。

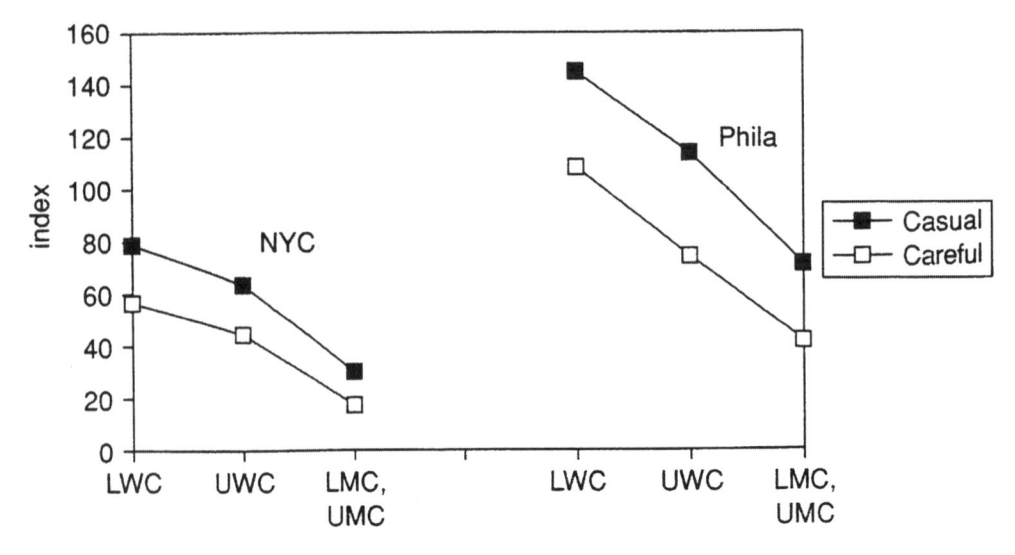

Comparison of New York City and Philadelphia[ð]patterns(Labov 2001:96)

(5) 次の例文を見比べて，非標準英語には，本文で触れた「二重否定」以外にどのような特徴があるか，説明しなさい。

    標準英語   非標準英語
肯定文： 1a. He knows something. 2a. He know something.
否定文： 1b. He doesn't know anything. 2b. He don't know nothing.
    1c. He knows nothing.   2c. He know nothing.

(6) 標準英語と比べて，アフリカ系アメリカ人日常英語（AAVE）では間接疑問文の作り方にどのような特徴があるか，説明しなさい。

  SE: I asked Mary if she could come.
  AAVE: I asked Mary could she come.

(7) 標準英語と比べて，アフリカ系アメリカ人日常英語（AAVE）では be 動詞と所有格の使い方にどのような特徴があるか，説明しなさい。

    SE   AAVE
    This is Bill's book.   This Bill book.
    This book is Bill's.   This book Bill's.（*This book Bill.）

いわゆる「黒人英語」という呼び名について

　本章では英語の社会的バリエーションを解説するにあたって，アフリカ系アメリカ人日常英語（AAVE）の例を多数取り上げた。アフリカ系アメリカ人というのは，祖先がアフリカから来たアメリカ人を指し，日系アメリカ人，ベトナム系アメリカ人，イタリア系アメリカ人，ドイツ系アメリカ人などと並ぶ呼称である。

　このエスニックグループに属する人々の日常英語が，発音・文法の両面で独特の特徴を有することはしばしば指摘されてきたが，言語研究の枠内で科学的に研究されるようになったのは1960年代に入ってからである。それ以前は標準英語との違いを表面的に捉え，「文法がない」「論理性が欠落している」といった否定的な評価を与えるのが普通だった。しかし40年間にわたる研究の結果，AAVEの時制や相，動詞の屈折体系は他の諸方言と同様に規則的で，その中には標準英語とかなり近い性格を有するものもあれば，大きく異なるものもあることが解明されてきた。1990年代末にカリフォルニア州オークランド市教育委員会が行った決定を発端として，AAVEの位置づけをめぐり，米国全体に論争がおこったが，これに対してアメリカ言語学会はいち早く声明を発表し，その規則性を明確にすると同時に，言語や方言を規範的な立場のみから扱う姿勢を戒めている。なお，この変種は，以前は黒人英語と呼ばれることが多かったが（p.115の図ではそうなっている），現在ではAAVEという名称の方が政治的配慮のある表現だとされている。上記の論争をきっかけに，一般にはEbonicsという名称も普及している。

Chapter 12 How English Is Acquired: Psycholinguistics

> **BASIC QUESTIONS**
> 幼児は特に教わらなくても，一定の年齢に達すると自然にことばを話すようになる。幼児は大人のことばの「真似」をして言語を身につけると考えられやすいが，本当にそうだろうか。人間はどのようにしてことばを獲得（習得）していくのだろうか。

FIRST LANGUAGE ACQUISITION

In Chapter 1, we pointed out how amazing it is that children can master their **first language** at an early age without explicit training. Do they learn their first language by imitating adult speech? Do their parents teach them how to form grammatical sentences? In this chapter, we will be concerned with how children acquire their first language.

first language ＝ 第一言語
imitate ＝ まねをする

PHONOLOGICAL DEVELOPMENT

Babies begin to utter sequences of sounds such as "ba," "ma," and "na" around their sixth month of life. This is called **babbling**. Interestingly, those who are going to become native speakers of English and those who will learn Japanese as their mother tongue produce the same sounds when they babble. Also, both hearing and deaf infants go through this stage in a similar way.

babbling ＝ 喃語（なんご）
mother tongue ＝ 母語

Data from fifteen languages show that [p b m t d n k g s h w j] are frequently found in babbling whereas [f v θ ð ʃ ʒ l ɹ ŋ] are not. Babbling increases in frequency until about the twelfth month of life, at which point children begin to produce their first words. Tables 1 and 2 list consonants that English-speaking children are able to produce by ages two and four, respectively.

stops	fricatives	other
p b m	f	w
t d n	s	
k g		

Table 1 Consonants at age two

stops	fricatives	affricates	other
p b m	f v		w
t d n	s z ʃ	tʃ dʒ	l ɹ j
k g ŋ			

Table 2 Consonants at age four

We observe the following tendencies in the two tables as well as in the list of sounds that frequently occur in babbling:

1. Stops are acquired before fricatives, affricates, glides and liquids.
2. Labials are acquired before sounds having other points of articulation.

Note also that [θ] and [ð] are difficult to articulate and are thus acquired late.

inventory = 一覧表

phonotactic pattern = 音素配列パターン

Not only is the sound inventory of children different from that of adults, but their **phonotactic patterns**, the patterns governing how one sound is combined with another, are different as well. A linguist named Neil Smith reports that his son consistently replaced [θ] with [f] (e.g. *thick→fick*). In Chapter 11, we saw that [θ] becomes [f] in Cockney (and [ð], its voiced counterpart, becomes [v]). [θ] and [ð] are systematically replaced by [f] and [v] in African American Vernacular English, too. Consider some examples.

(1) e<u>th</u>er → e<u>f</u>er   too<u>th</u> → too<u>f</u>
    bro<u>th</u>er → bro<u>v</u>er   smoo<u>th</u> → smoo<u>v</u>

The remarkable cross-linguistic similarity suggests that these replacements are not random but governed by a general principle.

consonant cluster = 子音連鎖

English permits a large number of **consonant clusters** such as [sp] (<u>sp</u>eak, e<u>sp</u>ecially, gra<u>sp</u>), [str] (<u>str</u>ong, a<u>str</u>ology), and [spt] (ga<u>sped</u>). Children often delete certain sounds to simplify consonant clusters, as illustrated by the examples in (2).

(2) <u>sp</u>eak → [pɪjk]   f<u>r</u>om → [fʌm]
    <u>sl</u>eep → [sɪjp]   bum<u>p</u> → [bʌp]

In the fast and casual speech of adult speakers, consonants are often dropped at the end of a word, yielding pronunciations such as *didn' wan' us* (< didn'<u>t</u> wan<u>t</u> us) and *the firs' chil'* (< the firs<u>t</u> chil<u>d</u>). Deletion of final consonants is frequently observed in children's speech as well.

(3) cat → [kæ]   bus → [bʌ]

By deleting a final consonant in examples like (3), children produce words that consist of a single open syllable (CV). This is the most common syllable pattern of human language.

MORPHOLOGICAL DEVELOPMENT

In Chapter 3, we examined how morphemes are put together to form words. When English-speaking children begin to produce their first words, these words seem to have no internal structure. They are mostly **monomorphemic**.

monomorphemic = 単一形態素の

(4) [dɑ] "dog" [mɑmɪ] "mommy"
    [ʃuw] "shoe" [nejm] "name"

Bound morphemes are absent and the child's entire vocabulary consists of free morphemes. As we know, English has many irregular noun and verb forms.

(5) Irregular Nouns   Irregular Verbs
    singular plural   present past
    deer   deer   put   put
    wife   wives   bring   brought
    man   men   run   ran
    datum   data   go   went

It is reported that children produce the correct irregular forms (*men*, *went*, etc.) at this stage, treating them as monomorphemic words. Later, when they realize that *men* consists of the two morphemes "man" and "PLURAL" and that *went* consists of the two morphemes "go" and "PAST," they start producing *mans* and *goed* by adding -*s* to *man* and -*ed* to *go*. In other words, children at this second stage generalize the regular plural ending -*s* and the regular past ending -*ed* even to words which have irregular inflections in adult language. This process, further illustrated in (6), is called overgeneralization.

(6) baddest (worst)   shelfs (shelves)
    freezed (frozen)   teared (tore)

After a period characterized by overgeneralization of the rules, children gradually learn the exceptions to those rules and begin to use the adult forms again—but this time, analyzing them as

bimorphemic, or containing two morphemes.

So far we have focused on the development of inflectional endings. How do children acquire derivational affixes? The word *teacher* consists of the base verb *teach* and the suffix *-er*, and the word *computer* is made up of the base verb *compute* and the suffix *-er*. Both cases of suffixation involve a change of category (verb → noun). Both also involve a change of meaning, but not in the same way. *Teacher* means 'person who teaches', while *computer* means 'machine that computes'. The *-er* of *teacher* is called **agentive** *-er*, the *-er* of *computer* **instrumental** *-er*. In child language, agentive *-er* emerges earlier than instrumental *-er*. **Productivity** and **semantic transparency** seem to determine the order of acquisition. Agentive *-er* may be added to any verb V to form a derived noun meaning 'person who Vs'; it is productive and semantically transparent. Instrumental *-er* is not as productive and may not be added to every verb.

SYNTACTIC DEVELOPMENT

When infants produce their first words, they utter these words to convey complex messages that would be expressed by a whole sentence in adult speech. Such utterances are called **holophrases**. Every child goes through this **one-word stage**. The words of this stage are used to perform various speech acts such as asserting ([dɑ] "There is a dog." or "I saw a dog."), ordering ([now] "Don't do that."), and expressing a desire ([bʌʔ] "I want up.").

Around the age of eighteen months, children begin to produce two-word utterances like those in (7). Since the two words are simply placed side by side, their meaning must be guessed from the context in which they are used.

(7) Hit doggie. (probable meaning: "I hit the doggie.")
Mommy water. (probable meaning: "Mommy is drinking water.")
Daddy sock. (probable meaning: "Daddy's socks")
Baby chair. (probable meaning: "The baby is sitting in the chair.")

Since the utterances of the **two-word stage** lack inflectional suffixes, it is hard to tell whether or not children at this stage have acquired syntactic categories.

two-word stage＝
二語文期

After the two-word stage, children begin to produce more complicated utterances, putting several words together.

(8) What that?
   Daddy like book.
   He play little tune.
   Man ride bus today.
   Me wanna show Mommy.

The utterances of this period look like "telegrams" in that they lack **function words** (determiners, prepositions, auxiliary verbs), words that show the relationships between the lexical words of a phrase or a sentence. This **telegraphic stage** lasts until the age of about three, when function words begin to emerge. As is clear from the examples in (8), children at this stage are able to form hierarchical structures like the ones produced by the adult grammar. It is generally believed that at this stage they possess syntactic categories and rules of sentence formation.

function word＝機能語

telegraphic stage＝電文期

Meanwhile, children learn more complex "rules" of grammar, such as the *wh*-movement and inversion that apply in question formation (Chapter 6). While adult language requires the application of both of these rules to produce questions like *Where do you go?* and *What can he play?*, the first questions produced by children tend to look like *Where you go?* and *What he can play?* Here, *wh*-movement has applied without inversion, a possibility that, in adult English, can appear only in **embedded questions** such as *I wonder what he can play*. Curiously, the opposite case of inversion without *wh*-movement does not seem to occur. That is, children do not produce questions like *Do you go where?* or *Can you play what*. In some sense, inversion seems to be more complicated, more difficult for children, than *wh*-movement.

embedded question＝
埋め込み疑問，間接疑問

SEMANTIC AND LEXICAL DEVELOPMENT

How do children acquire the meanings of words? Just as children make morphological errors as a result of overgeneralization, they may overextend (or underextend) the meanings of words at early stages of their linguistic development. **Overextension** occurs when children use a word for things to which it does not actually refer in adult language. For example, *bow-wow* may be used not only for dogs but also for all kinds of four-legged animals, and *daddy* may be used not just for the child's father, but for all men. **Underextension** occurs when a word is used for a narrower range of things than it actually designates. For example, a child may say *car* only when referring to his toy car, and not when referring to actual automobiles.

Since semantic development is closely tied up with general intellectual and cognitive development, it is natural to hypothesize that children master more general and basic words at earlier stages than complex and special words (the **complexity hypothesis**). If we compare the meanings of the two prepositions *to* and *into*, for example, we can see that the former is more basic than the latter. First, *to* is morphologically simpler than *into*. Second, *to* is less complex semantically, representing simply a goal or point of arrival, while *into* represents arrival at the inside of some three-dimensional space. Because of these differences, *into* takes more time for children to acquire than *to*. *Out of* is even more difficult than *into* because, although these two prepositions share the feature of three-dimensional space, *out of* also involves a "negative" feature which *into* lacks. If you go into a room, you are in the room. In contrast, if you go out of a room, you're <u>not</u> in the room any longer. The negative feature seems to be responsible for the relatively late acquisition of *out of*.

The complexity hypothesis also accounts for the relative order of acquisition of different senses of a single word. In Chapter 4, we saw that the concrete or physical meaning of a word (for example, *The rock <u>fell</u>*) can be metaphorically extended to an

---

overextension = 過大拡張

underextension = 過小拡張

complexity hypothesis = 複雑性の仮説

abstract, non-physical meaning (*His spirits fell*). If the abstract meaning really is an extension of the physical meaning, we have a natural explanation for the fact that children acquire the physical meaning first. Likewise, adjectives like *long* and *short*, whose concrete meaning refers to the spatial length of an object (*a long/short pencil*), are extended to the more abstract notion of temporal length, as in *a long/short time*. Because of this semantic difference, the spatial meanings are acquired earlier than the temporal meanings.

spatial＝空間の

temporal＝時間の

To sum up, we have seen that children acquire their first language through the following steps.

1. Babbling: up to about 10 months
2. One-word stage: one year to one year and a half
3. Two-word stage: one year and a half
4. Telegraphic stage (lexical words): around 3 years
5. Acquisition of function words, overgeneralization: 3 to 4 years
6. Adult grammar: about 5 years

THEORIES OF LANGUAGE ACQUISITION

So far we have examined how phonology, morphology, semantics, and syntax develop over the first few years of life. How can we account for this development, which results in an extraordinarily complex system of knowledge by about the age of five?

A simple and apparently natural hypothesis is that infants, more or less like parrots, imitate or mimic the language of their mothers and the other people around them. There are several problems with this hypothesis, however. Perhaps the biggest problem is what is called the **poverty of the stimulus**. The linguistic input that children receive from their parents and other speakers (both adults and older children) are insufficient to explain the knowledge of their language that the children come to possess. They are also insufficient to explain the process of overgeneralization, which we examined earlier in this chapter. Errors like *foots* for *feet* and *goed* for *went*, in other words, which invariably occur in the course of acquiring English, cannot be

mimic＝まねる

poverty of the stimulus＝刺激の乏しさ

explained on the basis of the child's linguistic input.

Such errors are not limited to the field of morphology. Here is an example from syntax. Adult speakers of English say *He put it on* (the pronoun *it* here referring to an article of clothing) rather than *He put on it. In the grammar of adult English, in other words, there is a rule which says that when **phrasal verbs** like *put on*, *take off*, and *take out* are used with a direct object pronoun, the pronoun must be sandwiched between the verb and the **particle**, as in *He put it on* or *He took it out*. Children never hear their parents or other people say *He put on it. Nevertheless, at the age of three or four, they often produce ungrammatical sentences like *They took out it or *He beat up him.

Such examples show that the imitation theory is not tenable (i.e. cannot be maintained). Since the grammar of a human language is highly abstract and complicated, it cannot be learned by simple imitation. Rather than imitating adults' language, children seem to attain the adult grammar as the result of an internally directed process of development, much in the same way that, for example, they attain the ability to walk on two feet. From a slightly different perspective, children are not passive receivers of signals from other speakers, but are active creators of their language. Since no nonhuman animals exhibit the capacity to acquire or create language in this way, it has been suggested that human beings are endowed with an inborn language faculty, an innate capacity to acquire language. This idea is called the **innateness hypothesis**, and in Chomsky's theory it is embodied as the **Language Acquisition Device** (LAD), often identified with Universal Grammar (UG).

```
┌─────────────────────────────────┐
│ Language Acquisition Device     │
│   = Universal Grammar (UG)      │  ⟶  adult grammar
└─────────────────────────────────┘
         ↗   ↑   ↖   ↖
   linguistic stimuli from parents and other people
```

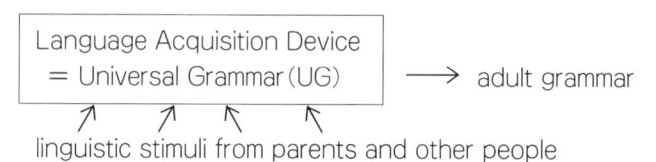

It should be noted that the innateness hypothesis does not claim that children can acquire their native language all by themselves.

Children must be exposed to language in order to activate the LAD and develop their innate capacity fully. Exposure to language can be compared to sprinkling water on plants in order to stimulate their growth.

Another important element related to the innate language faculty is the development of the brain. Several different pieces of evidence suggest that there is a **critical period** for language acquisition, which is closely associated with the period of brain and motor development. You acquired your first language without any difficulty. However, if you try to learn a new language at the age of nineteen or twenty, you will have a very hard time. It seems that after a certain age we lose the ability to acquire full command of a new language, even with explicit instruction and training. The critical period hypothesis is also supported by the rare instances in which children, as the result of abusive treatment, were denied access to linguistic stimuli during the critical period and failed to acquire language as a result.

critical period＝臨界期

motor＝運動神経

Although numerous studies have been carried out with the aim of gaining insights into children's acquisition of grammar, we still do not understand it fully. We can only hope that the combined efforts of linguists, psychologists, neurologists, and other researchers will enable us to unravel the mystery in the not-so-distant future.

linguist＝言語学者
psychologist＝心理学者
neurologist＝神経学者

Comprehension Check

✎ 空所を埋めなさい。

　　子どもは生後6カ月頃にはじめて言語としての音声を発するようになる。この時期に発する音声は（　　　　）と呼ばれている。生後（　　　　）頃に，最初の語を生成する。子どもが早い時期に発音できるようになる分節音は，言語にかかわらず共通している。この時期に子どもが発音する語の音節構造の典型は（　　　　）である。当初，子どもが生成する語は自由形態素のみからなり，（　　　　）はまだ見られない。この頃の語は，一語で大人の（　　　　）と同じような機能を果たしている。この時期を一語文期という。次の時期は生後18カ月頃に始まり，（　　　　）と呼ばれる。その後，子どもは3歳ぐらいまで（　　　　）のような文を生成する。この時期の文には（　　　　）がないものの，文法構造の面から見ると，大人とほとんど変わらないと言える。3歳から4歳ぐらいには，（　　　　）と呼ばれる間違いをよくする。しかし全体的に見れば，子どもは比較的短期間に，苦労せずに母語を獲得する。（　　　　）説によると，これは子どもには生まれつき言語を習得する装置が備わっているからである。

Exercises

(1) 次は幼児が発話した単語である。大人の発音と，どこが違うか説明しなさい。

desk	[dɛk]	small	[mɑ]
bring	[bɪŋ]	from	[fʌm]
bus	[bʌ]	sea	[tij]
thing	[tɪŋ]	go	[dow]
look	[wʊk]	room	[wuwb]

(2) 幼児が形態規則を習得しているかどうかを調べるために，よく使われる手法の1つに，無意味語を使った実験がある。以下の無意味語を名詞として提示し，複数形を作るように指示したとき，幼児はどのような形を作るだろうか（複数語尾-s, -esの綴りだけでなく，発音も含めて答えなさい）。また，それはなぜか，説明しなさい。

　　heaf　wug　lun　tor　cra　tass　kash　nizz

(3) 各組で，どちらの単語（または用法）が早く習得されるか見当をつけなさい。また，そう考える理由を説明しなさい。

　1. from / out of　　2. off / on　　3. big / small　　4. narrow / wide

5. from then on / from home　　　6. fall silent / fall down

(4) 次は一語文期および二語文期の子どもの発話例である。それぞれが，大人の英語ではどのような文に対応する可能性があるか，考えなさい。

<u>一語文期</u>
"Down."　　　　"Door."　　　　"Here."

<u>二語文期</u>
"John water."　　"Mommy sock."　"Doggie bark."

(5) 次は，日本人の1歳8カ月の男の子と母親の会話である。この子どもは言語習得のどの段階（時期）にあると考えられるか，根拠をあげて答えなさい。

母：あそこにトラック，置いてきたでしょ。
母：持って来て。
子：あ。（トラックを取り，こわれていることに気づく。）
子：お。
母：おかしいね，これ。
母：あそこの自動車，みんな持っておいで。
子：わあ。（他の車を取る。）
母：そう，そう。
母：ここ，並べて。
子：大っき(い)。（大きいトラックを取る。）
母：うん。それ，大きい。
子：大きい。（調査者にトラックを渡す。）
子：大き(い)。
母：大きいね。
母：これは。（小さいのを見せる。）
母：小っちゃい。
母：小っちゃい。
子：大っき(い)。

（出典　http://jchat.sccs.chukyo-u.ac.jp/JCHAT/akidata/AKI04.cha）

英語の分かるサル —— カンジ

　カンジ(Kanzi)は，アメリカのジョージア州立大学の研究所で育てられているサルの名前である。これは，ボノボ(bonobo)と呼ばれる類人猿の一種で，チンパンジーより人間に近い能力を備えている。研究者は，カンジが生まれてから何年もの間ずっと一緒に生活し，人間の幼児に話しかけるのと全く同じように英語で話しかけて，育ててきた。その結果，カンジは1,000語ほどの英単語を耳で聞いて理解し，また自分でも使えるようになった。だだし，口や顎，のどの構造が人間とは異なるから，自分で発音することはできない。しかしながら，口には出せなくても，頭の中では英語を理解していることが証明されている。これは，人間の乳幼児が，口では片言しかしゃべれなくても，親や兄弟が話すことばを頭の中で理解できるのと同じことだと言えよう。また，カンジの子どもも英語が理解できるようになった。ただ，これが「母語」の獲得と言えるのか，それとも，人間で言うと「外国語学習」(第二言語習得)に当たるのかは，議論の余地があるだろう。この実験の結果が，言語能力というものを人類だけの特質であるとするChomskyの主張に対して，「反証」となるのかどうか，興味深いところである。

　話を人間に戻そう。ある心理学者の研究によれば，人間の幼児は母親の胎内にいるときから既に母親のことばを聞き始め，また，生まれてからは，身振りや顔の表情が言語の習得に重要な役割を果たしているという。Chomskyの「言語獲得装置」が実際に人間の遺伝子に組み込まれているとしても，それが具体的にどのような刺激によって開花するのかを明らかにすることが重要になってきている。

Chapter 13 How English as a Second/Foreign Language Is Acquired: Applied Linguistics

> **BASIC QUESTIONS**
> 外国語の習得は，母語の獲得とどのように違うのだろうか。どのような要素が外国語の習得に影響するのだろうか。どのような過程を経て，外国語は習得されるのだろうか。

Second Language Acquisition

Although applied linguistics is a relatively new discipline with barely a 40-year history, it has quickly become a vast vibrant field of research. The chief area of interest for applied linguists is **second language acquisition** (SLA)—the study of how people who have already developed their first language (mother tongue) become proficient in their second, third or later language. SLA research tries to account for the many factors affecting this process. There are three main areas of interest: 1) characteristics of learner language, 2) influences outside the learner, and 3) individual differences among learners.

> second language acquisition ＝第二言語習得

Characteristics of Learner Language

The workings inside a learner's brain are not directly observable. By looking at what the language learners produce—what they say or write—and by asking them to report on how they learn, researchers have established the importance of L1 (first language, mother tongue) transfer and knowledge of Universal Grammar. **L1 transfer** refers to the incorporation of L1 features into the knowledge system of L2 (second or other language). It is different from translation, borrowing, and **code switching**. The amount of L1 transfer that a learner does is influenced by how near or distant he/she perceives that the L2 is from his/her native language.

> L1 transfer ＝母語の転移

Some **errors** occur as a result of L1 transfer. For example, if a Japanese speaker says, "I'm sorry" instead of "Thank you" when receiving a gift, he/she has made a transfer error by using L1 (Japanese) pragmatic knowledge to select an L1 expression すみません, which is then simply translated into an L2 (English) equivalent. As another

> code switching ＝コード切り替え（話している途中で１つの言語（あるいは方言）から別の言語（方言）に切り替えること）
> error ＝誤り（第二言語を完全に習得するまでの中間言語（interlanguage）における誤り。単なる言い間違いなどの "mistake" と区別される。）

example, learners usually learn that the meaning of *become* is なる and *come* is くる. However, they produce **become to do*, as a literal but incorrect translation of the Japanese phrase するようになる (*come to do*).

Other errors are neither purely L1 nor L2 forms; they are **creative constructions** caused by the overgeneralization, ignorance, or incomplete application of rules in addition to the faulty understanding of distinctions in the **target language**. For instance, a learner might learn the phrase *go to sleep* and then overgeneralize to produce **go to shopping* instead of *go shopping*. Another type of error is induced by faulty instruction. For example, a teacher might simplistically explain that *was* is a marker of past tense, and that *-ed* endings on verbs also mark the past. This might lead the learner to produce **Yesterday it was rained*. The intermediate stages of language a learner goes through before attaining a complete mastery of the target language are called **interlanguages** (IL).

Learner Progress

Although the study of learner errors is important, it only gives us one part of the language acquisition picture. The other part of the picture—what learners can produce correctly—has led to an understanding of **acquisition sequences** and **developmental sequences**. There is strong evidence that second language learners acquire morphological features in a fixed order and pass through a predictable sequence of developmental stages that is similar to the developmental path followed by children learning English as a first language. For example, the four distinct stages of development in the acquisition of English L2 negation are summarized in Table 1.

The first stage is characterized by negative particles (*no, not*, or unanalyzed *don't*) attached to a declarative utterance. This is followed by the second stage, in which the negative particle (*no, not,* or unanalyzed *don't*) is moved inside the utterance. By the third stage, the learner can attach a negative to **modal auxiliary verbs** but at first they might be unanalyzed formulaic chunks. In the fourth stage the negation

creative construction ＝
創造的構築

target language ＝
目標言語

interlanguage ＝中間言語
（目標言語を完全にマスターするまでの，誤りを含んだ中間的な言語体系）

acquisition sequence ＝
習得順序
developmental sequence ＝
発達順序

modal auxiliary verb ＝
法助動詞

Stage	Description	Example
1	External negation —*no* or *not* placed at head of utterance	*No speak English
2	Internal negation —*no, not,* or *don't* placed between subject and main verb	*Mai not play piano. *Keiko don't play piano.
3	Negative attachment to modal auxiliary verbs.	I can't understand.
4	Negative attachment to auxiliary verbs as in target language rule	She didn't heard it. He doesn't know anything.

Table 1 A developmental sequence for negation

rule has been acquired, although tense and number might still be marked incorrectly.

A learner's rate of error production often makes an inverted U-shaped curve, as in the figure below. At first, learners may avoid the grammatical structure or may be able to memorize a **chunk of unanalyzed language** that includes the correct form. In that case their error rate would be low. However, as the learner begins to use the structure more often, he or she will certainly make errors. After time and with practice, the errors will become fewer as the learner masters the form. The message to remember here is that ERRORS ARE GOOD; they are evidence of learning.

chunk of unanalyzed language＝分析的に捉えられていないことばの塊

Influences Outside the Learner

SLA researchers are also interested in how the physical and social environment surrounding the learner will affect language development. Age seems to be related with the ability to develop a native-speaker accent—if a learner begins before the early teen years, native-like accent is more likely. However, this does not explain why some learners in **immersion programs** and bilingual programs continue to produce non-native-like pronunciation even though they may have started language learning very young. This phenomenon has been seen in immersion programs in Canada and the United States as well as in Japan. In the early years (grades 1-3) the students begin producing native-like pronunciation and their grammar, vocabulary,

immersion programs＝イマージョン・プログラム，集中訓練（すべての科目で母語を使用せずに第二言語だけで授業を行う教育）

and language skills improve rapidly. From grade 4 onwards, grammar, vocabulary, and language skills continue to improve but the same students begin to produce L1-accented second language. One explanation may be that retaining an accent is a way for the students to protect their ethnic and cultural identity. They might fear that other members of their community would react negatively if they sound "too much like a native speaker" of the foreign language.

The effect of "natural" and "educational" settings on language learning is another area of interest. It has long been assumed that learners who are exposed to the L2 in a natural setting (i.e., learners living and working in a community that uses the target language for all aspects of everyday life) develop their language abilities by participating directly in interactions without the explicit attention to rules and language principles seen in educational settings. Furthermore, it has been assumed that learners in natural settings are able to attain higher levels of L2 proficiency than students who are exposed to the second language only in a classroom context.

However, recent research has shown that this is an overly simplified idea. For one thing, it is not unusual for learners in natural settings to consciously try to find opportunities to practice particular words and phrases and for them to privately keep a notebook, journal, or other records of vocabulary and informal rules. Such learners are not just being exposed to language; they are using learning strategies to make the most of this exposure. Additionally, there is growing evidence that **formal instruction** (classroom-based instruction of grammar) at the right time and in the right amounts may help some learners develop more grammatical accuracy than they would in purely naturalistic settings.

formal instruction =
正規の授業（授業できちんと文法を教えること）

Individual Differences among Learners

Another area of SLA research studies how the rate of L2 acquisition and the ultimate level of success can be affected by individual differences among learners. **Individual differences** (ID) research covers many interesting topics. For example, little is known about how a learner's beliefs (especially those of adult learners) affect language-

Individual differences =
個人差

learning behavior. Similarly, few studies have examined the causes and effects of anxiety and stress on learning and memory. Most ID research has focused on the following four areas: **language aptitude, motivation, learning styles**, and **learning strategies.**

Language aptitude is defined as the capability to learn language that is dependent on certain unchanging characteristics in a learner. In other words, aptitude research aims to find out if some people are born with more talent to learn foreign language than others. The research done up until now seems to show that language aptitude is distinct from motivation and intelligence. According to research using the Modern Language Aptitude Test (MLAT), four factors contribute to language aptitude: 1) **phonemic coding** ability (the ability to make a link between sounds and symbols and then code them in a way that they can be remembered later), 2) grammatical sensitivity (the ability to recognize grammatical functions of words in sentences), 3) **inductive** language learning ability (the ability to see patterns and relationships between forms and meanings), and 4) **rote learning** ability (the ability to make and remember associations between sounds, forms and meanings). Aptitude tests make it possible to design more effective teaching materials that capitalize on learners' strengths and compensate for their weaknesses. For example, if a learner is weak in phonemic coding ability a teacher could make listening tasks easier by supporting them with pictures and other visual aids.

Motivation, which most people agree is extremely important to language learning success, has also become a popular area of SLA research and may provide an important link between the fields of linguistics and psychology. There are many reasons why people might choose to learn a language: a desire to engage in the task of language learning for the sheer joy of doing it (**intrinsic motivation**) or the desire to engage in language learning for an external reward like a better job or a course grade (**extrinsic motivation**). Motivation is affected by person's self-image and by whether or not they believe they are capable of success. This is particularly important because it is normal in the course of language learning to experience setbacks

language aptitude ＝
言語適性（言語学習能力）
motivation ＝動機づけ
learning style ＝
学習スタイル
learning strategy ＝
学習ストラテジー

phonemic coding ＝
音素符合化

inductive ＝帰納的
rote learning ＝
丸暗記学習

intrinsic motivation ＝
内的動機づけ
extrinsic motivation ＝
外的動機づけ

and failures. Language learners with a mastery orientation tend to explain their failures as a lack of sufficient effort and look for ways to do better the next time. Setting and achieving realistic goals helps to sustain motivation: If a language learner experiences success he or she will want to continue and as the saying goes, "Nothing succeeds like success."

Conclusion

As we learned in Chapter 12, all children acquire their first language as the result of an apparently effortless course of phonological, morphological, syntactic, semantic and lexical development. In contrast, there are many factors that affect second-language learning. How much one already knows, how strategic one's learning is, how embarrassed one is about making errors, and so on, all affect second language learning. However, one message is clear: It is never too late to start learning a second language.

Comprehension Check

✎ 空所を埋めなさい。

　　応用言語学の中心は（　　）の研究である。学習者が目標言語を習得するまでには色々なことが起こるが，特に重要なのは，学習者の母語の特徴が目標言語の習得過程に直接に影響する（　　）と呼ばれる現象である。たとえば日本人はお礼を言うときに「すみません」と言うことがあるから，それが英語学習にも影響して，Thank you. の代わりに（　　）と言ってしまうといった誤りである。目標言語を習得するまでの過程は，学習者によってバラバラではなく，ある程度，一定の（　）がある。たとえば（　　）の習得過程において，助動詞にnotを付ける規則を習得する前に，単純に主語と動詞の間にnotやnoを置くという傾向が見られる。具体的な教育の場では，すべての科目を目標言語で授業する（　　　）プログラムや，ネイティヴスピーカーの母語習得と同じように日常生活の（　　）な環境でその言語を身につけさせる方法などが試みられているが，正規の授業で適切な時期に適切な量の（　　）を教えることも有効である。更に，第二言語習得の成否は学習者個人にもかかっている。学習者の個人差の研究では，（　　　），（　　　），学習スタイル，学習ストラテジーの４つの要素が特に研究されている。

Exercise

These are just a few examples of L1 transfer errors made by Japanese learners of English. In the correction column, fill in the blanks with one word each. Can you explain which Japanese word or concept might have been the source of each transfer error?

Error	Correction	Source/explanation of the transfer error
1. Please teach me your telephone number.	Please ( ) me your telephone number	
2. Every winter I like to play ski.	Every winter I like to go ( ).	
3. His family members are three.	( ) are three members in his family.	
4. The books in that library are many.	That library ( ) many books.	
5. I could enjoy the party.	I ( ) the party.	
6. I found out my keys.	I ( ) my keys.	
7. He was born 50 years before.	He was born 50 years ( ).	

著者紹介

影山太郎（かげやま・たろう）
兵庫県出身。
大阪外国語大学英語学科卒業。同大学大学院，英語学専攻修士課程修了。
南カリフォルニア大学大学院より言語学博士号取得（Ph. D.）。
国立国語研究所名誉教授（元所長 2009 ～ 2017 年），関西学院大学名誉教授。

デシェン・ブレント（Brent de Chene）
米国カリフォルニア州出身。
ハーバード大学より B.A.，カリフォルニア大学（ロサンゼルス校）より博士号取得（Ph. D.）。
アメリカで言語学の講師を 3 年間勤め，1981 年に来日。
現在，早稲田大学名誉教授。

日比谷潤子（ひびや・じゅんこ）
東京都出身。
上智大学外国語学部フランス語学科卒業。同大学大学院，言語学専攻博士前期課程修了。
ペンシルベニア大学より博士号取得（Ph. D.）。
現在，国際基督教大学名誉教授。

Donna Tatsuki（ドナ・タツキ）
カナダ出身。
トロント大学卒業。テンプル大学ジャパン大学院教育学博士課程修了（Ed. D.）。
神戸商科大学助教授を経て，
現在，神戸市外国語大学名誉教授。

ふぁーすとすてっぷす いん いんぐりっしゅ りんぐいすてぃっくす
First Steps in English Linguistics
— 英語言語学の第一歩 —

2003 年 4 月 15 日　初版第 1 刷発行
2004 年 4 月 15 日　2 版第 1 刷発行
2025 年 9 月 10 日　2 版第 18 刷発行

◎ 著者　影山太郎／デシェン・ブレント／
日比谷潤子／Donna Tatsuki

版元　くろしお出版
〒102-0084
東京都千代田区二番町 4-3
TEL　（03）6261-2867
FAX　（03）6261-2879
https://www.9640.jp/
印刷　シナノ書籍印刷

© T. Kageyama, B. de Chene, J. Hibiya, D. Tatsuki 2004

●乱丁・落丁はおとりかえいたします。本書の無断転載・複製を禁じます。

ISBN978-4-87424-277-3 C3082